Talking with Your Baby

Talking with Your Baby
Family as the First School

Alice Sterling Honig
and
Holly Elisabeth Brophy

Syracuse University Press

First Edition 1996
99 00 01   6 5 4 3 2

All photographs courtesy of the authors, Christine Morin, and Carol Swick and Bonnie Waite of the Consortium for Children's Services, Inc.

The Paper used in this publication meets the minimum requirements of American National Standard for Information Sciences—Permanence of Paper for Printed Library Materials, ANSI Z39.48-1984. ∞™

Library of Congress Cataloging-in-Publication Data
Honig, Alice S.
Talking with your baby : family as the first school / Alice
Sterling Honig and Holly Elisabeth Brophy.—1st ed.
p. cm.
Includes bibliographical references (p.   ).
ISBN 0-8156-0355-X (pbk. : alk. paper)
1. Interpersonal communication in infants.   2. Interpersonal
communication in children.   3. Infants—Language.   4. Children—
Language.   5. Early childhood education—Parent participation.
6. Child rearing.   I. Brophy, Holly Elisabeth.   II. Title.
BF720.C65H65   1996
649'.68—dc20   95-39045

Manufactured in the United States of America

Alice Sterling Honig, professor emerita of child development, College for Human Development, Syracuse University, is the author of *Parent Involvement in Early Childhood Education,* published by the National Association for the Education of Young Children. She authored *Playtime Learning Games for Young Children* and coauthored (with J. Ronald Lally) *Infant Caregiving: A Design for Training,* each published by Syracuse University Press.

Holly Elisabeth Brophy is completing doctoral work at Syracuse University. She has extensive experience as an early childhood educator and as a parent educator involved in a variety of early intervention and family development programs. In addition to her work with children and families, she has conducted workshops and seminars on issues surrounding child and family development at numerous local, state, and national meetings.

Contents

1. Talking with Your Baby   7

2. Your Baby Is Smart   10

3. How Language Grows   12

4. Why You Should Talk to Your Baby Even Though Baby Can't Talk Back   19

5. Talk with Your Baby at Home When You're Doing Chores   21

6. Things You Can Do and Say To Make You and Your Child Feel Happy   32

7. Tears, Fears, and Runny Noses   37

8. Potty Words for You and Your Child   41

9. How To Find Good Books for You and Your Baby   45

10. Snuggling with Books and Your Baby   56

11. Things You Can Do To Help Your Child Learn as You Read Together   59

12. Easy Songs for You and Your Child   64

13. Games for You and Your Child   75

14. Games To Give Your Child a Strong Body and a Strong Mind   81

15. Easy Toys You Can Make from Things at Home   85

16. A Sense of Humor with Funny Jokes and Silly Words   95

17. Imagination and Your Child   100

18. Does TV Help Your Child's Language Grow?   109

19. Good Things To Do with Your Baby When You're Not at Home   114

20. When Babytalk and Baby Play Embarrass You   119

21. What You Can Say When Your Child Says Words You Don't Want To Hear   122

22. How To Get Your Child To Do What You Want Without Getting Mad   124

23. Teach Your Child Words To Make Friends and Get Along with Other People   134

24. Things To Remember   143

25. Finding the Gifts of Your Child   145

Other Good Books To Boost Your Baby's Language   148

References   149

1 Talking with Your Baby

All parents are excited when their babies learn how to talk. Your child's first words are exciting. This book will show you that babies can "talk" to you even before they learn to say actual words. In the book you will find many easy ways to help your baby learn language, and you will learn how babies learn to talk.

Being a parent is a hard job, and sometimes you may feel tired or angry or even embarrassed if your baby or toddler starts crying in the store or on the bus. You will find a chapter in this book that talks about what to do when you have these feelings. You can find out how to get your child to do what you want without getting mad. You can find out what you can say when your child acts smart back to you or says things you don't want to hear.

Parents want their children to do well in school and to make friends. As a parent you can teach your child how words and actions help children to make friends and get along with other people. You can read about how to help your child become a better friend and playmate in this book.

Some children have many loving grown-ups around them like daddies, grandmas, grandpas, aunts, and uncles. Even though there are many important people in a child's life, this book is written with mothers and fathers in mind. Since both Moms and Dads will be reading this book, we will sometimes call a parent *Mama* and sometimes we will use the word *Daddy*. You might like other words

7

for mother like *Mom* or *Mommy* or other words for father like *Dad* or *Papa*. We are using the words Mama and Daddy, but if you like other words for parents, just think of the words you like best when you read this book.

In this book, we sometimes call babies *he* and sometimes *she* because we want Mamas and Daddies with girls and boys to feel good reading our book.

As you read this book, one thing to remember is that you are the *most important person* in your child's life. When your baby is born, she does not know much about living in a world with other people. She has so much to learn. Learning how to talk is one thing you can teach your baby. You have such an important job. You have the power to teach your child the actions and feelings and ways to talk he needs to know to grow up healthy, happy, friendly, and ready to learn well in school.

Whisper sweet nothings to your baby.

When you have a family to care for, you have very busy days. You may have a job, children to care for, other family members to care for, chores to do around the house, sometimes school work and job work. It is hard to find time to read a book. Your child's life and your life can be happier by reading about how to help your child grow well. If you don't have the time to read the book all at once, pick out a chapter you really want to know about and read it. Next time, you can pick another chapter.

2 Your Baby Is Smart

Many people believe that babies do not know anything when they are born. Actually, scientists who study babies tell us that babies know a lot even when they are only a few hours old. Babies are born knowing how to suck. If you put your finger or a nipple gently in your baby's mouth, he starts sucking movements. If you stroke your newborn baby's cheek, she will turn her head on the side you touch to search for the bottle or breast to suck. If you put your baby to sleep on her tummy with her face down on the mattress, she knows to turn her head to the side so she can still breathe. If your baby is older than a few months and you very gently lay a light cloth over his nose and mouth, he will turn his head and move his arms to try to move the cloth off of his face.

Your baby is born with many other *reflexes* or actions she will do automatically when something happens. For instance, when a newborn has her head to one side, often she will extend her arm on that side and bend her other arm upward. This "fencing" position helped her to fit comfortably in the curve of her Mama's womb before she was born! What are some other reflexes your newborn baby will show? Try doing the following things with your baby. Gently tickle your baby's nose—he will make a sneezing action to help him clear his nose. Gently touch your baby's palm—her fingers will ball into a fist. Lightly touch the inside of your baby's foot—his toes will curl inward. Stroke the outside of the bottom of your baby's foot—her toes will curl outward. Your baby is even born knowing how to make a kind of crawling movement. Push against the bottoms of your new baby's feet while she is laying on her stomach—she will start to make beginning crawling movements (even though it will be another six to ten months before she actually begins to creep or crawl).

Introduce a new toy to your baby lovingly.

Most babies act startled when they hear loud noises. Loud noises can be really hard on a baby. They cause jumpy, upset feelings. Try to imagine what your baby felt like when she was in her mama's womb. Imagine how safe and warm she felt. Imagine how quiet and secure the womb was, and how loud and scary the real world can be. Loud stereos, televisions, and screaming can be so scary to your baby.

Your baby comes ready to learn at birth, and *you* are your baby's *first* and *most important teacher!*

3 How Language Grows

The beginnings of language learning start even before your baby is born. Scientists tell us that babies can hear before birth. This is important for mothers and fathers to know when a woman is pregnant. Suppose a pregnant woman gets really angry and screams at someone. Then her body makes chemicals that go through her bloodstream. You may have heard the expression that something "gets your adrenaline pumping." When a woman is pregnant, these chemicals go straight to her unborn baby. If a pregnant woman is nervous or upset, then these chemicals make her unborn baby nervous and upset. That is why it is so important to try to learn how to share feelings and to solve arguments more peacefully when a woman is pregnant.

Babies are born preferring a voice they know, like a mother's voice or a father's voice. Right from birth, you baby *knows* you are special. He likes to hear *your* voice best of all. There have even been studies that show that if a mom reads a particular story or rhyme to her baby over and over before she is born, the baby will be able to tell that rhyme from another rhyme even when she is only a few days old. That is pretty amazing! A young baby will even kick at a crib bumper to set off *Mama*'s or *Daddy*'s voice reading a story instead of kicking at a crib bumper that sets off a stranger's voice reading.

As you get to know your newborn, you will learn to recognize different types of cries. A newborn baby cannot *tell* you what's bothering him. How does your baby let you know that he *needs* you? *Crying* is his way of telling you he needs *your help*. When a baby cries, he is letting you know he counts on you to care, to carry, to comfort. Some newborns sometimes cry more toward late afternoons. Babies cry when they are wet or hungry. A baby may cry because he wants his mama or daddy to pick him up and cuddle him. These different types of cries are your baby's way of talking to you and telling you how upset he feels. The message is: "Help! I feel miserable. Mama, I need *you* to help me feel better."

When your baby is crying and upset, sometimes the sound of your voice can calm him. Your baby likes your soothing voice best of all, and to hear your voice is very comforting. Other things you might try to soothe a crying baby are:

- give your baby a pacifier to suck
- rock your baby
- pat baby's back gently over and over
- hum or sing in a low tone to baby
- wrap baby securely in a blanket to make her feel cozy and safe
- reassure baby with loving words that you are trying to help him feel better
- carry your baby close to your body as you walk around.

Between the ages of about one to three months you will notice that your baby begins to make cooing sounds like *oo, goo,* or *ah.* He will also smile when you speak to him and laugh. Be very supportive of his attempts to talk to you. Tell him, "I like it when you talk to me. I hear you. I hear you. That's a nice sound you are making, oo, ah, mmm!"

Babies like it when people use a special tone of

voice when talking to them. This way of talking is called *motherese,* and you may already know it! Motherese means that when you talk to your baby, you talk in a higher pitch. You also talk more slowly and make the tone of your voice go up and down.

From about four months to six months your baby will enjoy playing with different sounds like *ba* or *ga.* You can really encourage your baby to make more sounds by using motherese and by looking at your baby and talking when he talks to you. Your baby also begins to respond to different tones of voices at this age. He will respond differently to a friendly voice than he will respond to an angry, loud voice.

Beginning at about six months of age, your baby will start to repeat some sounds over and over like *bababa.* This is called *babbling.* Your baby loves the look of your face. Put your face close to hers and watch and listen when she "talks" to you. When she makes a sound, make the same sound back to her, and wait for her to make the sound again. Think about how you talk to your friends. When you talk to a friend, you talk, then listen, and then talk again. You *take turns talking.* You can do the same thing with your baby. Turn-taking talk helps your baby learn language. Talking with your baby makes your baby feel loved. *You* are the one your baby counts on to be his *special talking partner.*

At about eight months of age, your baby will start babbling with different consonant and vowel sounds. She might say *bagidabu* over and over. In the next few months your baby will begin to use long strings of these sounds. It will sound like he is really trying to tell you something. Sometimes trying to figure out what your baby is saying to you is really hard. If you can't understand what your baby is saying, just say *mmm* or *uh-huh* very lovingly. This will send your baby a very important message: "I like for you to try to talk to me. Keep trying!" Between about nine and twelve months of age, your baby may try to make her first words. Some common words are *li* for light, *ki* for kitty, or *ca-kuh* for cracker. Often the most precious new baby "words" that make families happy are *dada, mama, papa,* and *nana.* These words show your baby is learning who his special people are.

Talk about what your baby is doing and enjoying,
like patting the plush kitten's tail.

The more you encourage your baby to talk, the more he will use sounds and then words. You are also helping baby to learn to feel good about himself by showing how much you love to hear him talk to you. As your baby is learning to talk, remember that different babies speak more at different ages. You may have one child who began talking at ten or eleven months, and another who may not have started until later. Be patient and encourage your baby to understand words such as the names for food like *apoo* for apple, *ca-kuh* for cracker, *nana* for banana, *yo-at* for yogurt, *poon* for spoon. Other early words are: *banky* for blanket, *shoe*, and *ha* for hat. As your baby learns a word, you want to make sure she knows what the word means. She may know how to say a word, but not know its meaning. For instance, if she says "shoe" and points to her blanky, she hasn't yet learned the meaning of the word *shoe*.

On the other hand, your baby may know what the object, shoe, is if you show it to him, but he may not know the word, *shoe*, to tell you. There is a big difference between knowing something in your mind and knowing how to say what that something is with words. These are two different language skills babies have to learn.

To help your baby learn words and their meanings you can make a game out of magazine pictures. Find pictures of everyday things your baby sees, like a cookie, a dog, a flower, a car, a glass of juice, a ball and so on. Say to your baby, "Show me the dog. Where's the doggie?" Show your baby the picture of the dog. Your baby will learn words much easier with games like this. If your baby points to the dog picture but doesn't say the word, don't worry. Just your baby pointing shows how much language you have been teaching him. Sometimes this game is easier if you first use real things like a ball or cracker or book to teach new words. Play naming games at every mealtime. Play naming games as you diaper baby or dress him. You can play naming games around the house and through the day.

After the first year of life, language continues to grow. Babies often use one word to stand for a thought. You baby might say *ki* and point to the cat.

This gesture and sound might mean "That's a kitty." Your baby might say *up* meaning "I want to be picked up."

During the second year of life, toddlers begin to put two or more words together. Your toddler might say *shoe on* for "Please put my shoe on," or she might say " *'tove hot"* to let you know the stove is hot. During this age, most toddlers leave out little words like *the* or *a*. Soon they will learn these words, too. You will notice that your toddler begins to use different tones to let you know that she is angry or scared or happy. A toddler uses different tones to *tell* you about something or to *ask* you for something or to *question* you when he feels puzzled. Listen for your baby's *tones* of voice even when she is still mostly babbling and not using too many "real" words yet.

As toddlers begin to learn the rules of language, like *how to use the past tense of a word*, they often apply those rules to all words. If your toddler falls down and hurts his knee, he might say, "I falled down" instead of "I fell down." He might say, "I hurted my knee" just the way he says, "I patted the kitty." You do not need to make a big deal out of correcting him. Just say, "Oh, you hurt your knee. Let's wash off your hurt knee. I'll find a band-aid to fix your sore knee." Be proud that he is learning rules about language. When something already happened in the past, our English language rules add an *ed* sound to the word, as in patt*ed* instead of pat. Your turn-taking talk has helped your baby figure out the "ed" rule! As your toddler learns the rules of language, he will correct any mistakes himself.

What about Baby Talk

You may want to know that it is fine to use baby talk with your baby. Babies really enjoy tacking an *ee* sound on to familiar words to make *doggie, eggie,* or *horsey.* When your baby reaches the toddler age, though, start pronouncing words in the right way. A baby may not be able to say *water* so *wa-wa* is fine. The *r* sound is very hard for babies. Other hard sounds are *s, th,* and *f.* Some babies say *'top dat* for *stop that* and *shishy* for *fishy.* These hard sounds become easier for toddlers to say. Say real words like *water* instead of *wa-wa,* so your baby can hear all of the sounds in the word. Hearing all the sounds makes learning how to say the word easier for her. Toddlers begin to learn new words very quickly. By the end of two years of age, toddlers know about 300 words. By the end of three years, they know 1,000 words, and by the end of six years of age, they know 8,000 words!

4 Why You Should Talk to Your Baby Even Though Baby Can't Talk Back

You know that babies can "talk" to their mamas and daddies even before they learn words by cooing and babbling to their loved ones. The more you talk lovingly to your baby, the more loved he feels and the more he wants to talk back and forth with you. Most babies will smile and laugh when a special adult smiles and talks to them. Try making your voice go up and down. Try cooing to your baby with a slightly higher pitch. Young babies seem to respond with more alertness to higher voice tones.

Talking early to your baby helps your baby learn about language. How you talk with your baby makes a difference in how well he uses language even years later! Scientists who study about children tell us that most children who use language well and do well in school have mamas and daddies who talked a lot to them when the children were babies.

Your baby learns how to make the sounds of language by listening to the sounds you make. He also begins to learn the names of things, people, and actions. Babies learn what different words mean as they listen to their special adults talk about an experience. Your child learns how to put words together to make

Your baby will love to hear you talking about an apple.
He knows how good it tastes.

sentences by listening to you talk in sentences. If you do not talk much to your baby, he will not learn much language. *You* are the most important language *teacher* for your baby.

5 Talk with Your Baby at Home When You're Doing Chores

You can talk to your baby anytime when you are doing work at home. Try to involve your child in everyday chores that you have to do. When you do chores at home, you are busy and probably in a hurry. Involving your child may seem like it takes too much time and is too much trouble. Taking time to talk to your child and letting her help is a little more trouble for you, but it is *important*.

Think of you and your child as a team, and you're the captain. You're the leader, the teacher, and you can share all that you know with your child. Your child loves you, and he wants to be with you and to help you. Think of what a loving, happy relationship you can have with your child by finding the time to make little moments in the day mean a lot.

Talking During Cleaning and Washing Time

Even simple chores like putting a spoon next to the plate as you set the table or tossing some dirty clothes into the washing machine make your toddler feel proud to be your big helper. These chores teach your child about thinking, about talking, about using language, and about being with other people. Experts

21

tell us that these skills are important for a happy, smart future for your child.

Cleaning at home gives you many chances to talk to your baby. Tell your baby what you are doing: "I'm cleaning. Yes, I'm cleaning. I'm going to make our house clean." As you wipe off spills say "I'm washing off your hi-chair." As you clean the floor say, "I'm sweeping the crumbs off the floor."

Your young child can help you polish the furniture with a rag. Tell your child exactly what to do. Say, "Help me polish the table leg. Right here. Rub your cloth up and down, and up and down. We're wiping all of the dust away." Many cleaning products are poisonous so give your child a plain, clean rag to use. Be sure to keep your cleaning supplies safely out of your child's reach on a high shelf. Tell your child what a wonderful job he is doing and how clean the table looks. Your child will feel so happy and proud if he thinks that he's helping you! Young children love to feel important.

Your work in the family seems like the most important job in the world to your baby. That's why your baby wants to do what you do! Babies love to bang with pots and pans because your pots and pans are important in your family for cooking and for feeding everyone.

Teach your child about the words that you use in cleaning. Your child will begin to learn new words like *polish, sweep, dust, mop, dirty, clean, wipe, scrub, shiny, wet, damp,* and *dry*.

Teach your child *describing* words or *feeling* words when you are working together. Describing words are words like *smooth, bumpy, rough, soft,* and *hard*. As you and your child clean a table say, "The top of this wooden table is *smooth*. Feel how *smooth* it is. Now *feel* our carpet. Our carpet is *bumpy*. It's not *smooth* like the table." Soft things in your house would be things like a cotton ball, a fluffy dishtowel or a pillow. Rough things could be a dish scrubbing pad, sandpaper, the bristles on a toothbrush, the bristles on a hairbrush, or the cement sidewalk. Hard things would include a table, the floor, the door of the refrigerator, the chair, the bathtub (it's smooth, too), and the wall.

An activity like washing the dishes after supper is a real learning experience for your child. You will need a low bench for your toddler to stand on in order to reach the sink and help in your washing up dishes. Make sure that you are standing right behind your toddler or beside him with your arm around him so that you can help to steady him as he stands. Toddlers sometimes lose their balance and you want to be able to catch your toddler if he slips.

Think about all of the steps in washing dishes and the *order* of the steps. Help your child understand the order. *First,* you have to *scrape* the food off the plates, *then* you have *wash* them with soap and water. *Next,* the dishes have to be *rinsed. After that,* dishes are *dried.* The *last* thing to do is to *put away* the dishes. These kinds of activities where children have to think about what comes first and then second and so on help children's thinking skills grow. Figuring out the order of the actions helps their minds grow. All of these things help your child get smarter! Both you and your toddler may get a little wet and need a sponge mop to clean a puddle on the floor, but think of how much your baby is learning! Think of how proud he feels that he is helping you do something important in your family.

Babies love to help you wash up.

Talking During Cooking and Food Shopping Time

When you are fixing lunch for your toddler say, "You're hungry. I'm fixing a sandwich for you. Now I'm cutting the bread. Now I'm spreading the jam. Strawberry jam. Yum Yum! It's almost ready. You're waiting so patiently. Here's your sandwich. It's ready!" This kind of conversation helps your hungry, irritable toddler stay in control until the food is ready!

Your toddler or young child will have great fun helping you put groceries away. Grocery time is a wonderful chance for your child to build his vocabulary and learn new words. He learns about different kinds of food. He learns how to sort different kinds of foods. Explain to your child, "Some foods need to stay cold. They go in the refrigerator. Some foods like cereal boxes and cans can stay on a shelf." Ask your child to find all of the cans in the grocery bag and put the cans together on the table. Ask your child to find the cold things and put the cold things together on the table. Teach your child about different fruits and vegetables. As you put away the fruit, label the items for your child. "Here are the yellow bananas, and the red apples."

When you make a grocery list, your older toddler or young child may enjoy making a "list" too! Give your child some paper and crayons and ask him to "help Daddy make a list of food we need to buy." Your child will feel like he is Daddy's helper. This is a great way to include your child in household routines. Since your toddler will be hard at work making wavy line scribbles, ask your child to *tell* you the kinds of foods she wrote on her list. "Reading" a toddler's precious scribbles is tough! All of these activities are important for children to learn to read and use language. Making a grocery list helps children understand that writing has a purpose. They can see how writing is related to spoken words and how writing can be used for a shopping list!

Talking During Mealtimes

Mealtimes are language-rich times, too. Even though it is sometimes hard to find time to sit down and have lunch or supper together, this is really important to your child. Making time for eating together shows your child how important you think eating together is. A mealtime is also a great time for your child to learn new words. Think of all of the words your child learns from you at mealtimes. Talk about words like *plate, fork, spoon, cup, glass, table,* and *chair.*

Talk about the food on the plates. Describe how different kinds of food look. Try saying things like:

- "Your mashed potatoes are *warm* and *white.* They stick to your spoon."
- "Your ice cream is *creamy, cold,* and *sweet.*"
- "Your applesauce is *lumpy, bumpy,* and *cool.*"
- "Your crackers are *bumpy, crunchy,* and *salty.*"

Describing words, or *feeling* words, like lumpy, bumpy and cool are important words for children to learn.

Mealtime is a time to "recap" the day. Remembering or recalling things is good practice for your child's mind. Remembering involves language. Give your child a lot of help at first. Ask, "What did we do at the store this morning?" or "What kinds of food did we buy when we went shopping today?" or "What did we have for breakfast this morning?" A fun way to play this game is to give your child a real hint and a funny, silly hint. Say, "Did we have cereal for breakfast this morning or shoes for breakfast?" He will giggle and your funny question will jog his memory. As your child gets better and better at this game, make the hints a little harder. Say, "Did we have cereal for breakfast this morning or pancakes for breakfast?"

Sometimes older babies feel happier about mealtimes if they can feed a parent some food. Letting your baby feed you might be messy, but your baby will enjoy feeding his special adult. After messy mealtimes babies certainly don't like to have their faces washed. Language can be your secret helper to make washing your baby's face easier for both of you. Tell your baby, "Time to wash up now," as you bring the washcloth over to your baby. Talking helps to make

Babies enjoy feeding themselves.
Babies enjoy feeding you, too.

your baby ready to have you wash her face. As you gently wash her face, talk softly to her. Say, "I'm washing the food off your face. Washing the carrots off. Washing the potatoes off. There! A precious, clean face!" Say the same kinds of things as you wash his hands. Talking as you are washing your baby helps keep your baby entertained so he doesn't fuss.

Talking During Dressing Time

Help your child look through his drawers at home to see all of the different kinds of clothes. Give your child a pile of clothes from your laundry basket and help him put all of the socks together, all of his underwear together, all of his pants together, and all of his shirts together. He can help you put his clothes away.

Dressing your child in the morning is another activity for talking. As you dress your child, talk about what you are doing. Say, "We're putting on your shirt. First it goes over your head. Where's your head? There it is! Peek-a-boo! Now, put one arm through the hole. Now, the other arm. Now, we pull the shirt down over your pretty tummy. There, all done!" Saying loving things to your child like "pretty tummy" makes him feel special and adored. Think about all of the things you are teaching your child just by putting on a shirt. You are teaching your child the word *shirt*, and you are teaching your child the names of body parts like *head* and *arm*.

You are also teaching your child about the sequence of putting on a shirt. You can do the same sort of thing with pants, shorts, hats, gloves and other types of clothing. Try using time words with your child like *first, next, before, after* and *last*. Ask your child, "Do we put on your socks *first* or your shoes *first?*" Understanding the order of things is hard for young minds. Ask your child, "Do we take our pants off *before* we go to the potty or *after* we go to the potty?"

When you are helping your child dress, talk about the actions involved. For example, after your child has her feet in the pant legs, tell her, "Now, pull your pants up. Pull the pants over your legs." By doing this, you are teaching your child what the word *pull* means. Your child is also learning to act out the steps in dressing so over time she can learn to dress herself after a lot of practice and with your help and encouraging words.

Talking During Laundry Time

When you do laundry, your child can help you sort different kinds of clothes. Even a two-year-old can feel proud to help put the shirts in one pile, the pants in one pile, and the socks in one pile. Talk about socks for your feet, pants for your bottom and your legs and so on. Your child can also help you sort colors. Ask your child to find all of the red things. Your child can sort dark and light colors, too. Use time words in doing laundry. Tell your child, "*First*, we sort the clothes. *Next*, put them in the washer. *After that*, we add the soap. *Last*, we turn on the washer."

When the clothes are dry, ask your child to help you find the *big* shirts and the *little* shirts. Size words are important for your child to learn. These words are fun, too! With these activities, you are showing your child that he is a big helper. Your child is learning to sort items by how big or little they are. He can find clean clothes from different groups like socks or towels or panties.

He can even learn about the textures of clothes. Some clothes feel *smooth*. Some materials, like terry-cloth, feel *rougher*. Laundry time is a good time to use describing words like *smooth* and *rough*. Other good describing words are *wet* and *dry*, and *cool* and *warm*. Let your child feel the *cool, wet* clothes *before* you put them in the dryer. Have your child feel the clothes *after* they are taken out of the dryer. The clothes feel *warm* and *dry*. Use words like *before* and *after* to help your child learn about time ideas. Learning the difference between *before* and *after* is a hard job for young children, so give them lots of practice by using the words yourself.

Your child is also learning about the order of things. She is learning new words like *soap powder*,

A laundry mess provides a happy
peek-a-boo time for a baby.

washer, dryer, spinning, wet, fold, corners, and
wrinkled.

Laundry time is a special opportunity for your toddler to feel proud of being a helper. Picking out the
matching socks to make a pair is a hard job. This job
helps your toddler "be a good detective" in looking
for a long sock of the same color or a short sock with
stripes on it. *Matching* socks is a game that sharpens
your baby's mind.

At the laundromat, entertain your child by talking
about the kinds of clothes he's wearing today. Is he
wearing pants or shorts or a shirt or a sweater? If there
are other children in the laundromat, what are they
wearing? Talk about colors here, too. Your child may
even be amazed by watching the clothes spin around
and around in the dryer.

Why Your Child Says and Does What You Do

You know that you are the most important person in your child's life. Your child *watches you* and *learns from you*. You are a teacher or a *model* for your child.

Lots of times children who are playing house pretend to drink coffee. This is because they've seen their parents drink coffee.

You may have particular mannerisms that your child has learned from you. For example, if you scribble and doodle on your paper as you talk on the telephone, you may notice that your child does the same thing when she pretends to talk on the telephone. You have *modeled* a behavior, and she is copying it.

As a parent you have to be careful to model the rights kinds of things. Children often copy *everything* they see you do, good or bad. If you curse when you're angry, your child will probably curse when he's angry. He won't know what he's saying. He'll just know that saying those words is what *you* do when you're mad. If you act angry toward other family members such as the baby's other parent, the baby will become tense and upset. He will also copy your angry voice. Try to keep *separate* some of your strong, unpleasant feelings toward some people and your baby's needs to have positive, loving voice tones from you.

6 Things You Can Do and Say To Make You and Your Child Feel Happy

Every diaper time, bath time, and bedtime can be a chance for some loving talking time with your child. Times like this can make you and your baby feel happy and secure.

Diaper Time

When you change your baby's diaper, take a moment to look in your baby's eyes. Let your voice be loving and warm. You will notice that your baby's eyes will light up, and she may giggle, laugh, or smile. Take a moment to kiss her toes and talk to her, "I'll kiss your toes. Mmmm. Lovey toes. Yum yum yum." Tickle her stomach or kiss her fingers. Tell her what you are doing, "I'm giving you a clean, dry diaper, love. Yes, all clean!"

Bath Time

Bath time is a playful learning time. As you bathe your child, talk about different body parts. Say, "Where are your toes? Here they are! Soapy toes. Clean toes!" Play with the water, "Splish, splash, we're taking a bath. Going to wash your fingers!

Where are your fingers? Where are they? There they are!"

Kids will look right up at you as you talk
about soapy bubbles and playing in the tub.

Invent fun bath games to help your child learn the names of body parts. Give your child a washcloth and say to her, "Where's your knee? That's right. Wash it! Where are your toes? That's right! Now wash them!" As he gets better at this game, you can try using two body parts. You might say, "Ears and toes" or "bellybutton and knees." Another time you play the game, try having *him* tell *you* to point to different body parts. Sometimes point to the wrong body part and see if he'll catch your mistake.

Bathtime is a great time to talk about *wet* and *dry*. Hand your child a washcloth and say, "Here's a *dry* washcloth. We put the washcloth in the water. Now the washcloth is *wet*" When your child gets out of the bathtub say, "You're all dripping *wet*. Here's a towel. I'll pat, pat, and pat and wipe all the water off. Now you're *dry*."

Try giving your child toys like a sponge and plastic cups to use in the bath. Say things like, "The sponge is full *of water. Let's squeeze* all the water out of the sponge. Help me *squeeze* the water out." When you use the word *squeeze,* squeeze the sponge so your child will understand what the word means.

When your child is playing in the tub with the plastic cup and water, tell him the *words* for his actions. Say, "You are *filling* the cup up with water. Now the cup is *full*. Now you're *pouring* the water out. Now the cup is *empty*." You give your child word power. He hears the words that belong with his actions.

You can even give your child books for the bathtub! Many books for children are made of vinyl or soft plastic so if they get wet, you can easily dry them off with a cloth. Check at garage sales or the grocery store for soft books.

Sometimes a Daddy or a Mama feels silly playing these games at first. Just remember that you are smart because you are reading about how to make your child smarter. What you are doing helps her to have a better life. You are doing things with your child that have been proven to help children learn language well and to help children feel good about themselves.

Bedtime

Bedtime is a special time for you and your baby. Try to have a routine that you use every night. When your child is familiar with the same bedtime routine, he feels more secure and he will go to bed more easily. One routine might be brushing teeth, changing diaper, or using the toilet, then snuggling with your child in a chair or in a bed for a few stories or lullabies.

Your child will probably enjoy picking out a favorite story to read. This could be his job every night. A favorite story could be a book or a story you have made up for your child or even a story you remember hearing. When you are reading stories, read by a soft lamp rather than an overhead light. You want bedtime to be a cozy, calm time for your child. Your local library has some good books to read at bedtime. Try some of these books:

- *Anno's Peekaboo* by Mitsumasa Anno
- *Mooncake* by Frank Asch
- *Ten, Nine, Eight* by Molly Bang
- *Martin's Hats* by Joan Blos
- *Goodnight Moon* by Margaret Wise Brown
- *I Like Me!* by Nancy Carlson
- *Five Little Monkeys Jumping on the Bed* by Eileen Christelow
- *Tomie DePaola's Mother Goose* by Tomie DePaola
- *Are You My Mother* by P.D. Eastman
- *First Pink Light* by Eloise Gilchrist Greenfield
- *Ben's Trumpet* by Rachel Isadora
- *The Snowy Day* by Ezra Jack Keats
- *Pet Show* by Ezra Jack Keats
- *Growing Colors* by Bruce McMillan
- *Whose Hat?* by Margaret Miller
- *Say Goodnight* by Helen Oxenbury
- *Ba Ba Sheep Wouldn't Go To Sleep* by Dennis Panek
- *The Little Engine That Could* by Watty Piper

- *The Wheels on the Bus* by Harriet Ziefert
- *A Pocket for Cordoroy* by Don Freeman

You can find picture books at garage sales for very little money. Remember that babies love the same book read over and over. They like the same songs sung over and over.

Bedtime is also a good time to talk about things that happened during the day. One expert on children suggests saying to your three-year-old child, "Tell me three things that made you happy today." Many times the things she will remember will be the loving things you did for her during the day like kissing a boo-boo, playing in the bath together, or baking cookies together. Quiet time together at bedtime is a peaceful way for you to end the day with your child.

7 Tears, Fears, and Runny Noses

Your young child is just learning about talking and what kinds of words to use in different situations. When a child is scared or hurt or angry, putting those feelings into words is hard. There will be times when you need to give your child the right words. In a way, you are talking *for* your child's feelings.

When You Have To Leave

Imagine that your young child begins to cry when you are about to leave. Your child may be afraid of being left without you. Help your child to express her feelings. You might say, "I know you feel *scared* and *sad* when I have to go, honey." Make sure you tell your child, "You are *safe* with Grandma (or Grandpa, your neighbor, or your child care provider.)"

Make sure that you tell your child when you will come back. Just saying, "I'll be back soon." is too hard for toddlers to understand. They don't know what *soon* means. Say something like, "I'll be back after your naptime and then we'll play." Say you will be back after your job is over, or after you buy food at the store or after you see the doctor. Telling your child what you will do together when you come back helps your toddler feel safe. She feels safe because she knows what is happening. You aren't just leaving. You're coming back and then you and your child will play with the blocks, with the pots and pans, with a doll, with a ball or a truck, and so on.

When you say things like, "I know you feel sad when I leave," you're telling your child that you understand how he feels. When you tell your child the two of you will play later, you're giving your child something else to think about besides your leaving.

Keeping Promises

Keeping promises to your child is *very important*. Keeping promises helps make your child feel safe and secure. If you promise you will read your child a story when she wakes up from nap, then make sure you read a story. If you promise your child you will play with the blocks when you come home, then make sure you play with the blocks.

Promises help children to think through the future. Knowing what will happen helps children build trust. Your child will feel so safe and happy knowing that she can count on you. When you keep promises you help your child to trust you and know what to expect from her world. Your child learns to treasure your words when you keep your promises to your child.

Boo-Boos

You can use language to comfort your child in other situations, too. Think about a time when your child has scraped a knee or cut a finger. It hurts to scrape your knee. Your child needs to know that you understand that she hurts. Even when a scraped knee seems like a little hurt to a grown-up, it may seem like a big hurt to a little child. Try saying something like, "I know it hurts to scrape your knee. I'll put a band-aid on it gently." When your child is hurt, he may need to be cuddled and held. Don't be afraid that you'll spoil your child by holding him. You can *never* give your child too much love and affection. Sometimes the words, "Come let Daddy (or Mama) kiss the boo-boo" work like magic. *Your* words and kisses soothe hurts just like a magic potion.

Babies need a hug and soothing words
when they are grumpy and upset.

Try to remember to talk to your children many times during the day. If you give your child a glass of juice, say "Here's your glass of orange juice" rather than just handing your child the glass and saying,

"Here." If your child has a runny nose, talk to your child as you get a tissue rather than just wiping the nose without a word. You might say, "You've got a runny nose today. Let me wipe your nose with a tissue. I'll wipe it gently. Your nose will feel better." Repeating a word like *nose* helps the child learn what the word means. *Nose* is a hard word for a baby to learn because he can't see his own nose. A word like *toes* is easier to learn because a baby can see and point to her own toes.

8 Potty Words for You and Your Child

Learning to use the toilet can be a very hard time for both you and your baby. Potty training is one task that babies need to be allowed to learn at their own pace. Try to be patient and flexible while your baby is learning to use the potty. Your patience will make things easier for you and your baby during toilet learning, which can sometimes take quite a while.

Is Your Baby's Body Ready To Be Potty-Trained?

There are nerve cells that run from your child's brain all the way down to the muscles that control the opening and closing of the bladder for pee and the opening for poop to come out. When the nerve cells are fully developed and covered with a special covering called "myelin," then they can send the message that the bladder is full and your toddler needs to pee or that he needs to poop. If these nerve cells aren't ready yet, then they can't send a quick message to your child's brain saying, "Get to the potty, fast!" That is one reason why potty training may be hard for many children. Children may be 2 years old before their nerve cells are ready to carry quick messages that allow your toddler to controls his muscles in order to poop or pee at a certain time in a special place. If your toddler doesn't know when he has to go

41

An early stage of toilet learning is just
getting used to a potty and a toilet.

to the bathroom, then his body isn't ready for learning
how to use the toilet.

Sitting still can be so hard for toddlers, and this
makes toilet learning hard. Before parents start potty
training their child, the child should have the attention span to sit still for quite a while. Different children take different amounts of time to learn to sit
still. Forcing a child to sit still will be an impossible
job for you and your toddler. Wait until your toddler's
attention span has grown before you start potty
training.

When your child can sit still, increase her patience
on the potty by helping to entertain her. When she

sits on the potty, put a big stack of books right next to her so she can look through books while she's waiting to poop or pee. Try singing or doing finger-plays with your child. *Toilet time should be a relaxing, non-threatening time. It shouldn't be an angry time.*

Bathroom Words for Your Child

Words like *urinate* and *bowel movement* are too hard for young children to say. Many families use *pee* and *poop* as bathroom words because they are easy for toddlers to say. Before you start potty training, your child needs to have some bathroom words like pee and poop or other bathroom words that you choose for your child. Language will help your baby to learn to use the potty. Language will help your toddler understand your explanations of the potty and what you want your toddler to do.

Be Positive and Patient

Try to be very warm and loving as your child is learning to use the potty. Shaming a child and blaming a child for toileting accidents makes him feel embarrassed, unloved, and insecure for years and years to come. Give your toddler time to be potty trained.

Sooner or later, all children learn to use the potty. Some children may be 3- or even 4-years-old before they are toilet trained. *This is one of the most important periods in your child's development. Give him the time to learn so the experience will be a happy, positive one.* When you are warm and loving, he will want to please his special adult! This will help the toilet learning process.

Don't Gush and Flush!

When they have finally learned to use the potty, toddlers are *very proud* of the poops and pees they make. Making poops and pees is hard work for a little one. Give your toddler lots of praise for her hard work! Tell her, "You worked so hard to make that poop! I'm so proud of your hard work!"

Make sure that you don't flush away her work right away. Praising her for her work and then making her work disappear right away can be confusing for a toddler. It is perfectly normal for toddlers to be amazed and very interested in their poops and pees. Leaving poop and pee in the potty for a minute or two may seem strange to a grown-up, but it may be important to a toddler. For one thing, the loud sound of the toilet and the swirling water can be scary for a young child. Seeing poop and pee disappear immediately after such hard work could be disappointing for a toddler. Wondering if *they* might fall in a toilet and be swooshed away is a very real fear for many toddlers. When the potty is ready to be flushed, let your toddler take charge of flushing the toilet by pushing down the flusher handle.

9 How To Find Good Books for You and Your Baby

Reading to your child from infancy onward is one of the most important things you can do to help your child learn language. Experts who study about how children learn to use language and how they learn to read tell us that reading with children at home is a big part of a child's success with language and reading later in school. We think books are so special that the next few chapters are all about finding good books, snuggling and reading with your child, and teaching your child as you read together.

Read at home to help your child grow more and more interested in books and in wanting to learn to read later on. Reading is a skill your child needs throughout life. Hook your baby on books *early*. You want your child to have a passion for books. Some young children love to pick up a book, turn pages, point to pictures, and babble sounds seriously long before they use words.

Read with your child whenever you can, every day, if possible. Find a way to set aside time for reading, and you may find that a cozy book time together becomes a favorite part of the day for you as well as for your child.

Reading to a young baby may seem strange at first since a baby can't even talk yet, but reading to a baby

Get your baby enthusiastic about
pointing out pictures to you.

is important. Reading is important because you are
spending precious time with your baby. This makes
your baby feel loved and safe. You are showing your
child what language is and how to use language by
talking and reading. Your baby will not understand all
about language when she is only a few months old,
but as you keep reading, your baby's knowledge of
books and language will grow. Your child will grow
up with reading as a part of what families do together.
Here are some tips for finding books for babies:

- Choose books that are made of oilcloth, soft
  cloth, or plastic because babies like to put
  things in their mouths. Soft vinyl or plastic
  books are great for the bathtub!

- Choose books that are made of sturdy cardboard. These books can stand up by themselves so your baby can gaze at the pictures in the crib. Thick cardboard pages are also easier for little hands to turn. Cardboard books are easy to wipe off with a damp cloth if they get dirty.
- Choose books that have bright, clear pictures. One picture on each page is best. Too many pictures on one page or pictures full of a lot of details can be too confusing for a baby.
- Choose books that have pictures of things babies will find familiar. Babies will be interested in pictures of animals, babies, clothes, foods, and pictures of familiar faces. Some baby books have a "mirror" page made of a shiny material so baby can see her face!
- Choose books with a simple, short story. Many books for babies are labeling books. For example, on one page you may find a picture of a baby and the word *baby* written below it. *Friends* by Helen Oxenbury is a board book with one picture and a label on each page. *What Is It?* by Tana Hoban is a board book of actual photographs of everyday objects your baby will know, like a bib, a cup, a shoe, and a sock.

You will want to choose different kinds of books for your toddler or young child. Here are some things to remember when choosing books:

- Choose story books with predictable endings. In these books, it is easy to tell just what's going to happen. Your child can become very involved in the story if she can guess what will happen next.
- Choose stories with repetition. In these books

the same words or sentences are said over and over again. These types of stories often add character to character. For example, in the story *The Little Red Hen,* the hen keeps asking the animals to help her make bread. Each animal has a turn to say no: "Not I, said the dog." "Not I, said the cat." and so on. Children learn these stories very quickly, and then enjoy saying the story as the grown-up reads.

• Choose books that have a rhyming story. A rhyme is when two words end in the same sound like hat, cat, fat, and sat. Rhyming books by Dr. Seuss are wonderful and dearly loved by many children. Children like to play with rhyming words, and these stories are easy to learn. Stories like *The Cat in the Hat* and *Green Eggs and Ham* are classic children's stories.

• For younger children, look for books with bright, clear pictures without too much detail. If a picture is full of all kinds of small details, the child may become "overstimulated" trying to look at everything. In other words, there is so much in the picture, the child does not know what to look at first. A child could become very frustrated with this type of picture. Helen Oxenbury is a wonderful illustrator of many books for young children. Her pictures for children's books are simple, cheerful and warm. Look for children's books that have warm, loving pictures. Look for pictures that make you feel happy; they will probably make your child feel happy too.

• Choose books that have a nice story. You might want to look for books about being friends, or about a family. Arnold Lobel wrote a children's book called *Frog and Toad Are Friends*. Frog and Toad are friends and the some of the stories in the book describe things friends do for each other. You might want to find a book that teaches a message like the importance of honesty or of being kind and helpful. Many of the Berenstain Bears books, written by Stan and Jan Berenstain, teach lessons to children about honesty, about getting along with brothers and sisters or about being a friend. *The Berenstain Bears and the Truth, The Berenstain Bears Get in a Fight*, and *The Berenstain Bears and the Trouble with Friends* are a few books in the series. Berenstain Bear books are too hard for toddlers but they are usually very popular with preschoolers and young children.

Often, your child will want to read books about a popular cartoon character or action hero from television or about the characters from a movie. Lots of times you will see books about movie and TV characters in the grocery store or variety store. These books are OK but you can find other books that have better pictures, better stories, and good lessons for your child.

Here some books good to read with babies less than a year old:

- *Baby's First Picture Book* by George Ford.
- *Baby's Friends* by Neil Ricklen. Neil Ricklen has written a series of books for babies with photographs of babies and their special people, babies and their homes and babies' clothes and toys. Look for the following: *Mommy and Me; Daddy and Me; Grandpa and Me; Grandma and Me; Baby's Clothes; Baby's Home.*

- *Aleksandra, Where Is Your Nose?* by D. Christine Salac.
- *Gobble, Growl, Grunt: A Book of Animal Sounds* by Peter Spier.
- *Pat the Bunny* by Dorothy Kunhardt.
- *I See* and *I Touch* by Rachel Isadora. These books have wonderful descriptions of ordinary items that babies can see and touch in their homes and neighborhoods.
- *The Very Hungry Caterpillar* by Eric Carle (boardbook).
- *Puppy Says 1,2,3* by Joshua Morris. Each of Morris's books have a surprise squeak toy that babies will love to push and squeeze!
- *Babytalk* by Erika Stone. A collection of photographs of babies and toddlers doing everyday activities like looking, sleeping, playing peek-a-boo, and laughing. Simple word descriptions accompany each picture.
- Many toy companies such as The First Years make soft, vinyl books featuring objects like airplanes or animals that are great books for babies.
- Look for cloth activity books that give babies something to do like lift a cloth flap or feel a fluffy sheep or shake a rattle. *Snuggle Time* by Discovery Toys is a fun-filled book for babies.
- Also by Discovery Toys, the *Let's Look Book*, a vinyl book of bold black and white patterns and faces, appeals to young babies.

Here are some good books to read with babies between one and two years old:

- *Thump, Thump, Rat-a-tat-tat* by Gene Baer.
- *Max's Bath, Max's Bedtime, Max's Birthday*, all by Rosemary Wells.

- *Things I Like To Eat* by Zokeisha.
- *Anno's Faces* by Mitsumasa Anno.
- *Dressing, Family, Friends, Playing, and Working*, all by Helen Oxenbury.
- *The Baby's Catalogue* by Janet and Allen Ahlberg. A book about all of the things a baby knows about, like diapers, a crib, and special people.
- *Fluffy Bunny: A Soft and Furry Boardbook* by Demi.
- *Who's Peeking?, Who's Hatching?, Who's Mommy Is This?*, all by Charles Reasoner. These sturdy board books have wonderful sliding pages that reveal surprise pictures.
- Take a look at the *Poke and Look* book series produced by Grosset and Dunlap. These books examine everyday items like toothpaste and toilet paper in brightly colored illustrations. The books are filled with interesting holes your baby will love to touch and to poke.
- *Goodnight* by Dessie and Chevell Moore. This bedtime boardbook is beautifully illustrated with rich colors.

Here are some good books to read with your two- or three-year-old:

- *The Checkup* by Helen Oxenbury. A book about visiting the doctor.
- *Tickle, Tickle* by Helen Oxenbury.
- For toddlers and young children who are showing an interest in toilet learning, try the following books: *Once Upon a Potty* by Alona Frankel and *Sam's Potty* by Barbro Lindgren.
- The Pippo books by Helen Oxenbury. There is a series of books about Pippo and his experi-

ences, like *Pippo Gets Lost* and *Tom and Pippo and the Washing Machine.*

- *Is It Red? Is It Yellow? Is It Blue?* by Tana Hoban.
- *Push, Pull, Empty, Full: A Book of Opposites* by Tana Hoban.
- *The Hole Book* by Suzy Kline. A book with holes for toddlers to poke their fingers through.
- *Autumn Days* by Harold Roth. A sturdy cardboard book with real photographs of children and autumn activities like playing in the leaves, picking apples, looking at pumpkins and so on.
- *I Make Good Music; My Doll, Keisha; Big Friend, Little Friend; Daddy and I* by Eloise Greenfield.
- *Where's Baby Bear?* This is a turning picture book by Peter Seymour.

Here are some good books to read with children three years old and older:

- *Why Mosquitoes Buzz in People's Ears* by Verna Aardema
- *Stina* by Lena Anderson
- *The Great Kapok Tree* by Lynn Cherry
- *The Very Hungry Caterpillar* by Eric Carle
- *Jamberry* by Bruce Degan. A funny rhyming book.
- *Strega Nona* and *The Legend of the Bluebonnet* by Tomie DePaola
- *A Cake for Barney* by Joyce Dunbar
- *In the Tall, Tall Grass* by Denise Fleming
- *Wilfred Gordon McDonald Partridge* and *Possum Magic* by Mem Fox
- *Is Your Momma a Llama?* by Deborah Guarino. A rhyming book.

- *The Wind Blew* by Pat Hutchins
- *Brother Eagle, Sister Sky* by Susan Jeffers
- *Rain* by Robert Kalan
- *Can I Keep Him?* by Steven Kellogg
- *Brown Bear, Brown Bear, What Do You See?* by Bill Martin, Jr.
- *Chicka Chicka Boom Boom* by Bill Martin, Jr.
- *Make Way for Ducklings* by Robert McCloskey
- *I Can't Get My Turtle to Move* by Elizabeth Lee O'Donnell
- *Curious George* by H. A. Rey
- *Nursery School* by Harold Roth. A cardboard book about going to nursery school or childcare. The book has real photographs of children building with blocks, painting, looking at books, and so on.
- *Annabelle Swift, Kindergartner* by Amy Schwartz
- *Horton Hears a Who* and *The King's Kittens* by Dr. Seuss
- *Caps for Sale* by Esphyr Slobodkina
- *Lyle the Crocodile* by Bernard Waber
- *Harry the Dirty Dog* by Gene Zion

Places to Find Books

Your community has many resources for finding books. Check around at dollar stores, second-hand bookstores, and garage sales for inexpensive books. Store listings can be found in the yellow pages of the phone book. Look in the yellow pages under *Books* for a listing of second-hand book stores. Many second-hand books are $1.00 or less, and you can find some great books if you look in used bookstores.

Applying for a public library card is a wonderful way to find the best in children's books. Borrowing library books is free. Choosing the books can be a great adventure for you and your child. Librarians can help you choose books. The library will have a list of children's books that have won awards. These books are usually very good for children so you might want to start by looking at some of them.

The application for a library card is short and easy to fill out. The librarian will help you if you ask for help. Find out about it today! Look in the phone book under *Library* to find the address and phone number of your local library. Even if you do not have a library card, public libraries usually offer free story hours during the week. Sometimes they have weekly reading programs for babies and young children.

Making Up a New Story for a Picture or Book

Sometimes you find books that have pictures you like but stories you don't like. You can always use the pictures and make up your own story. Look at what is happening in each picture and make up a story to go with the actions. If you live in a neighborhood with people from many different lands, you may find books written in a different language. You don't have to read the words. Just make up your own story to go with the pictures. Picture labeling is a fine way to get babies and toddlers interested in books.

Some books for babies and very young children have no words, only pictures. *Shopping Trip* by Helen Oxenbury is a wordless book about a baby and her mother going shopping. Make up a story about going shopping or talk about what is happening in each picture.

You can also *make up your own stories to go with magazine pictures.* Check with friends, relatives, neighbors, social service offices, or medical clinics to collect and save old magazines for you. Look for different types of pictures: pictures of people, animals, objects. Point to a picture and ask your child to tell you what is happening in the picture. Make up a short story from one of the pictures, and tell it to your child. The story can be short. Your older child can help you make up stories.

You can also use the magazine pictures for sorting games. Ask your child to put a stack of pictures in piles that belong together, such as: animals, people, furniture, things that take you places like cars, trucks, planes, buses, bicycles, and so on.

Babies will especially enjoy looking at family pictures and photo albums. Show your child pictures of other family members to help him build the idea of what a family is. Tell your child stories about when you were a baby. Tell her about things you remember doing with your mama or daddy or aunts or uncles. Show your child his baby pictures, and tell him stories about when he was a little baby.

Family photo albums are also a good link to you when you're away. Your child feels much happier looking at your picture while he's waiting for you to come home. While you are out, leave some pictures with your child care provider to look at with your child. Seeing your family pictures will help your child feel more secure.

10 Snuggling with Books and Your Baby

Reading with babies should be a warm, loving time. Find a quiet time in the day for just you and your child. Be sure the TV is off or try to find a spot where you can't hear the television or the radio. Snuggle in a big, soft chair, or on the sofa, or in a bed. Being physically close to your child is as important as the words you will read. Snuggling with you will make your baby feel loved and safe. This is also a time when your child can show you how much he loves *you* by snuggling up to you as you read!

When you read to your child, read *slowly*. Think about how slowly you like to enjoy your favorite kind of ice cream cone. A book is just like a delicious ice cream cone. Take time to let your baby enjoy the sound of each word. Let him enjoy the pictures and the colors on each page.

As you are reading, watch what your child is doing. How could you know if your child is paying attention to the same part of the book you are? One thing you can do is look at his eyes. Is he looking at the same picture you are? If he isn't, he might be looking at the picture on the opposite page. Sometimes a picture is so interesting to a child that he takes a long time to look at the picture. If you notice that your child is really interested in a picture, go back to that page and look at the picture again with him. Ask a two- or three-year-old, "What do you see in that picture?" You will

Talk about books and pictures with your baby.

probably need to help him label the objects in a picture. You might say, "Oh, you're looking at the doggie. Woof! Woof! A furry doggie." Do this for babies too, but use fewer words. Try pointing to the picture and saying, "Doggie. Woof! Woof! A doggie."

Your child can give you clues about how to read the book. If your child is looking at all of the pictures very closely, read very slowly. Take lots of time to read each page. Look at the pictures. Talk about the pictures.

Exaggerate the words in the book. Make your voice go up and down when you're reading. If the words say the dog barked, "Woof," then make your voice a little deeper as you say, "Woof! Woof" Use different tones by changing your voice to go up and down. This makes the book more fun for you and your baby. Sometimes Mamas and Daddies think they sound silly when they first start reading to their children using funny voices. Your voice may sound strange to you. Lots of times we feel silly when we try something new. The more you snuggle and read with your baby, the easier and the more fun it will become for you. Snuggling during book reading time may become one of your favorite parts of the day with your child! You need the rest time too!

11 Things You Can Do To Help Your Child Learn as You Read Together

Once you have found time in the day to read, after lunch or just before bedtime or anytime, try to stick with that time. Young children like a routine that happens every day. It helps them feel safe and secure. Routines can also provide opportunities to learn about time. For example, if you always read a book *before* bed, you can help your child understand the concept of *before* and *after*. Try saying things like, "We have story time *before* you go to sleep" or "It will be bedtime *after* we read stories together." You can also talk about past and future time by saying things like, "We read that story *yesterday*. Would you like to read it again *today*?" Sometimes children pick out more books to read than can be read at one storytime, so try saying, "It's bedtime *now*, but would you like to save this story for *tomorrow*?" In addition to teaching a time concept, this technique works very well because it puts the child in charge of ending storytime by picking out tomorrow's book and finding a special place to keep it until then.

The more routine you make a reading time, the more likely you are to remember to do it every day. Reading can be a fun thing for you and your child to do together! This quiet time is also a great time for your child to tell you about her day. Encourage her to talk about day care, a friend, a picture she drew. Let your child know that what she has to say is important to you and that you want to listen to her.

When you are reading with your baby, you probably won't get through a whole book. Your baby may be more interested in crumpling the soft book in a fist or hand. Babies also love to put things in their mouths. This is one way babies learn about things. Babies cannot ask "What is this?" or "What does it do?" so they learn about things with their hands, and mouths, and eyes, and noses. They touch things, rub things against their faces, and try to eat them! Don't worry if your baby tries to chew on her vinyl or plastic book! If you don't finish the words in a book, don't worry. Your baby is still hearing you talk. He is handling the book. These are great ways to learn.

As your baby gets older, he may have a favorite book. One 15-month-old baby we know had a favorite book about animals. Each page had a picture of an animal. The animal name was printed below the picture. This baby loved to point to each picture and try to say the name or the sound the animal made. She would often point to the cow picture, say a loud "Moooo," and then break into giggles! As you teach your baby about a picture, you can begin to ask her "What's that?" If a book has a picture of a chair, say "It's a chair. A chair." If you have a chair in the room, show your baby the chair, "Here's our chair."

As you read a story to your older toddler or young child, you may find that your child wants to look at one page for a long time instead of turning the page after you have read the words. Think of your child exploring a book. Your child may see something on that page that is new and exciting to him. Something has really caught your child's interest! Encourage your child to talk about the picture. Try saying, "Tell me what you see in the picture," or "Tell me *all* about this picture." We know that children need practice talking and using language, and this is a great way to practice.

You can also talk about something *you* did that the picture reminds you of. If the book has a picture of an apple, you might say, "That's an apple. What did we have for lunch today? Yes, we had apples. What did we do with apples the day we drove out to the farm in the country? Remember? We picked apples off the apple trees. What did we do with the apples when we got home? What did we make with the apples? We made . . . apple . . . sauce! Right! We made apple-sauce." Questions that make children think about what has happened in the past are very hard for young children. These kinds of questions really sharpen your child's mind. Give her time to think about the question, but be ready to give her a hint if she's having trouble. One kind of hint is to give her part of the answer. This will help her remember and fill in the rest of the answer. This is the kind of hint used in the example about applesauce. We said, "apple . . ." and the child remembered applesauce.

As your child learns more words, you can ask harder questions about a book. You might ask, "What's he doing in the picture?" or "What's going to happen?" Ask your child to talk about the story. You might say, "What did you like about that story?" or "How did that story end?" These last two questions are hard so you might try asking them to your three-or four-year-old.

Some kinds of questions make children think more than other kinds of questions. Imagine there is a picture of a dog in a book. A question like, "Is that a dog?" makes the child answer either yes or no. The child doesn't have to do a lot of thinking. He might even guess the right answer without really knowing the picture is of a dog. Why would a question like, "What animal is that?" be a better thinking question for a child? With this question, the child can't answer yes or no. She has to think about all of the kinds of animals she knows. Her brain has to do a lot of work by sifting through what she knows about animals.

If your child is looking at a picture of children playing, try asking, "What are the children doing?" Use an interested voice as if you really feel glad that your child can explain things to you. Children love to tell grownups things. Your child will feel happy and proud to think he is teaching you something! When your child tells you about the children in the picture, he may tell you about the children on the slide or the children who are swinging. He must think about what he sees, and he must think about the words he needs to use to tell you about the picture. Thinking questions like the one above are called *open-ended* questions because they have more than one right answer rather than "yes" or "no."

Pictures in books can help children learn about feelings and emotions. Look at the people in the pictures. Look at the expressions on their faces. Ask your child, "How are the people feeling? Look at the smiles on their faces. They sure are feeling happy." Other pictures may show different feelings. If the picture shows someone crying say, "Look at his tears. He is feeling so sad." If the picture shows someone with wrinkled, knitted eyebrows and a frown say, "Look at her frown. See how her eyes and eyebrows are wrinkled. I think she's feeling angry." Talking about how people look when they are angry, sad, worried, and happy help children learn about feelings. Talk with your child about what makes him mad, happy, and sad. This helps your child learn about feelings.

Children love to hear the same stories over and over again. Hearing the same story over and over makes your child feel happy and confident. He thinks, "That's my story. That's the story my Daddy reads me!" When your child gets to know a story very well, he will begin to say the words with you.

12 Easy Songs for You and Your Child

Children love music and singing. Even babies as young as eight or nine months old are delighted by rhythms like "Hickory dickory dock. The mouse ran up the clock." When you do rhythms like this with your baby, exaggerate the sounds and speak slowly and almost to a beat. Try clapping your hands softly when you say it. For example, you would clap at the beginning of the words *hickory, dickory, dock, mouse, up, clock.*

Singing is an easy, free activity for you and your child. It will help your child learn more about words and talking. By two years of age toddlers can memorize as many as five different song melodies like "The Itsy Bitsy Spider" song. Your child will think your voice is the most gorgeous voice in the world, so don't worry if you think you can't sing too well! Here are some old-timey songs you and your children can sing together:

- "Old MacDonald Had a Farm"
- "The Hokey Pokey"
- "If You're Happy and You Know It Clap Your Hands"
- "London Bridge is Falling Down"
- "Where is Thumbkin?"
- "Ring Around the Rosy"

- "The Itsy Bitsy Spider Climbed Up the Water Spout"
- "Row, Row, Row Your Boat"
- "Twinkle, Twinkle, Little Star"
- "Jingle Bells"
- "A Tiskit, A Tasket" (a green and yellow basket)

Sometimes a cousin can introduce
a baby to making music.

If your child is in childcare, she may know some songs you can sing together. Check with your childcare provider for some songs. You can also check out children's music tapes from the public library. Some libraries may check out tape-players too.

There are several popular singers for young children like Ella Jenkins, Hap Palmer, and Raffi. Your child may know some of these songs from day care. Check your public library for music cassette tapes by these singers. Many of Ella Jenkins' records and cassettes for children encourage children to clap their hands, stomp their feet, and march to the music.

Hap Palmer's record *Pretend* encourages children to use their imaginations by pretending to be different animals. *Movin'* by Hap Palmer is collection of different kinds of music. Some of the music is very slow, and some of the music is very fast. Children can learn to listen better by listening to the different tempos and speeds of music. Check out this record or cassette and let your child dance to the speed and beat of each song. As you play each song, help your child learn to listen. Say to your child, "This song is slow. How does the music make you feel? How do you want to move when you listen to this song?"

Raffi sings very popular songs for children like "Baby Beluga," "The Corner Grocery Store" and "All I Really Need." Raffi sings traditional songs that many children know like "This Old Man," "Kumbaya," and "Swing Lo, Sweet Chariot." Music is great fun for toddlers. One 19-month-old had particularly enjoyed the song "The Itsy Bitsy Spider" on a tape. With the first note of music, she would give a huge grin, bounce her bottom up and down, and wave her arms.

Singing with Your Baby

Don't be afraid to be silly when you're singing. Before you know it you'll be having great fun! Use hand and body motions when you sing. Actions help babies learn a song. For example, when you sing "The Itsy Bitsy Spider," act out the spider climbing up the water spout by putting your opposite thumbs and index fingers together and "climbing" upward. When you sing the "Down came the rain and washed the spider out" line, make a motion of rain falling down. When you sing, "Out came the sun and dried up all the rain," make a big, round sun with your arms.

Try making your voice go up and down when you sing with your child. Make it exciting. The more excited you are, the more your child will want to learn the words and to sing with you. Toddlers enjoy songs when other children and grown-ups join in the singing.

Action Songs

Babies and young children love to use their bodies to move in songs. Try singing "This Little Piggy" while you pretend that each of your child's toes is a "piggy" (start with your child's big toe). Here are the words: "This little piggy went to market. This little piggy stayed home. This little piggy ate roast beef. This little piggy had none. This little piggy cried, 'Wee Wee Wee,' all the way home."

Another good song to sing with your child is Miss Polly. Here are the words and body actions to the song: "Miss Polly had a dolly [fold your arms together as if you're holding a baby] who was sick, sick, sick [swing your folded arms back and forth]. So she called [pretend you are dialing the telephone] for the doctor to come quick, quick, quick. The doctor came with her bag [hold out your hand as if you were holding a bag] and her hat [touch your head], and she knocked on the door [pretend you're knocking on a door] with a rat-a-tat-tat. She took one look and then she said,

Getting together with other families
for singing and play with kids.

'Now, Miss Polly put her straight to bed' [shake your finger as if you were giving some very important advice]. She wrote on her paper [pretend you're writing on paper] for a pill, pill, pill. I'll be back in the morning with the bill, bill, bill."

Even babies eight or nine months old enjoy games with body actions like "Pat-a-cake." Here are some motions to try: Hold your baby's hands and clap them together as you say "Pat-a-cake, Pat-a-cake, baker's man, bake me a cake just as fast as you can. Roll it" [slowly roll your baby's hands round and round], "and pat it and mark it with a B" [trace a B on your baby's tummy with her hands], "and put it in the oven for baby and me!" As you say the last line , use a happy voice as you bring your baby's hands together and pretend to put the cake in the oven.

Fingerplays are fun for toddlers and young children. Try doing "Open, Shut Them." Start by holding both hands open in front of you. Sing "Open, shut them," [close your hand into a fist when you sing "shut them,"] "Open, shut them. Give a little clap," [clap your hands together] "and put them on your head," [put your hands on your head]. Try using different body parts like head, cheeks, mouth, nose, feet. You can end the song by singing "Open, shut them. Open, shut them. Give a little clap and put them in your lap."

Another song about body parts is called "My Thumbs Are Starting to Wiggle." Try singing or chanting, "My thumbs are starting to wiggle, wiggle, wiggle," [wiggle both thumbs] "My thumbs are starting to wiggle, round and round and round." [Move your thumbs in a circle.] Try different body parts like head, feet, arms, or elbows.

"Little Red Wagon" is a great action song for children. This song is about an imaginary wagon that is broken. The child pretends to fix the wagon with different tools like a hammer, a screwdriver, a wrench, a mallot, pliers, and so on. Each time you sing the song, use a different tool and pretend to use that tool. For instance, when your child pretends to use a hammer, have her move her arm up and down as if she were hammering. Here are the words to the song: "Bumping up and down in my little red wagon, bumping up and down in my little red wagon, bumping up and down in my little red wagon. Can you fix it for me? Kanesha's [your child's name] going to fix it with her hammer. Kanesha's going to fix it with her hammer. Kanesha's going to fix it with her hammer so we can go for a ride!"

"Head and Shoulders" is another song that lets your child learn body parts and move around to use a lot of extra energy! As you sing about a body part, you touch that body part. Here are the words: "Head and shoulders, baby, one, two, three [clap each time you say one, two, three]. Head and shoulders, baby, one, two, three. Head and shoulders, head and shoulders, head and shoulders, baby, one, two, three!" Try other body part combinations like ears and eyes, elbows and knees, toes and nose, stomach and neck, and so on. Try singing faster, then slower. Try making your voice get louder or softer. Lots of young children love this song! Relax and have a good time with your child. Before you know it, you and your child may be dancing the afternoon away!

Singing To Soothe Your Baby

Young babies love to listen to soft singing. Songs like "Rock-a-bye Baby" have been used by parents for years and years. Sometimes when you are so tired from holding your crying baby you can hum two tones to make a soothing sound for your baby like "Ah-uh, Ah-uh, Ah-uh." Humming the tune over and over can help your baby fall asleep.

Using your baby's name in a made-up song makes him feel loved and safe. You can choose a simple tune to go with your made-up words. Sing the words over and over. If your child is tired and fussy, hold him tenderly and sing, "Tyrell [baby's name] is sleepy. Tyrell is sleepy. It's time for him to sleep. It's time for him to sleep. I'll snuggle Tyrell in his crib. It's time to go to sleep."

Sing your baby's name woven into your song over and over and over. Babies love to listen for their names. You can make up songs to go with any activity in the day from naptime to dinnertime.

When To Start Singing with Your Baby

Right from birth, your baby loves the sound of your voice. Sing softly to your newborn baby. Sing as you are changing her diaper. Sing as you are dressing her. Sing anytime. The sound of your voice is a wonderful gift to your child.

Sometimes people feel embarrassed to sing. They think they can't sing very well. Remember that to your baby, your voice is the most beautiful voice in the world. As your baby gets older and hears the songs over and over, he will slowly try to copy the songs you sing. He will try to learn your songs!

Use songs that you remember singing as a child. Use songs that are songs of your people and your culture. Using songs special to you will make the songs even more special to your child.

Chants

Children love chants. The next time you go to the store, try using a chant like "We're going to the store, the store, the store!" Clap your hands as you chant. When you're waiting at the bus-stop, try a chant like "We're waiting for the bus, the bus, the bus. We're waiting for the bus so we can home!" A chant like this can make the wait a little easier for both you and your child.

You can make up chants and songs with just two notes. Choose any two notes you can manage. Here are some songs and chants to sing:

"Sally Go Round"

[Hold hands with your child and go in a little circle as you do for ring around the rosy. When you sing

"Boom" gently tumble down to the ground. Toddlers love this song! They love to tumble down at the sound of "Boom!"]

> Sally go round the sun
> Sally go round the moon
> Sally go round the chimney tops
> Every afternoon. . . . BOOM

"The Wheels on the Bus"

> The wheels on the bus go round and round [Draw a circle in the air]
> Round and Round, Round and Round
> The wheels on the bus go round and round, all through the town.

Other verses to try are:

> The doors on the bus go open and shut [Bend your arms and then move them out to each side *(open)* and then together in front of you *(closed)*]
> The lights on the bus go blink, blink, blink [make a flashing action with your hands]
> The people on the bus go up and down. [stand up and sit down]
> The driver on the bus says 'Please move back.' [motion backwards with your hand]

Let your child make up some verses when he feels ready.

You can use chants anytime. Try using chants when your hungry toddler is waiting for dinner to be ready. Chant "Making dinner. Cooking carrots. Pouring milk. Making dinner. Soon we will eat." This kind of talking will help your toddler stay in control. It will reassure her that you know she's hungry and that you're preparing food and are going to feed her soon.

Use chants to help your child get ready for a change in a daily routine. Try using chants to help your child get ready for clean-up time if you need to leave soon on an errand. Hearing that he will have to clean up helps your child prepare to stop his play and clean up. Try using chants while you're dressing your child. Chants which use the same words over and over help children to focus on *what* will happen, *when* it will happen, and *how* it will happen. A child can't make a change very quickly like a grown-up can. Children need time to think about change such as getting ready for bed. Your words get your child ready for a change. Words help your child feel comfortable so he can make the change successfully.

Rhyme Games

Most children love playing with rhyming words. Even babies rhyme silly, nonsense words like *oogy woogy poogy*. Make up a rhyming word game. First, explain to your child what rhyming words are. Rhyming words sound alike. They have the same ending sounds. Say some rhyming words for your child like *bat-mat-rat* or *nose-rose-toes*. Say an easy word like *feet*, and ask your child to think of a rhyming word like *meat, eat* or *seat*. Have your child say a word; then you find a rhyming word; and then your child can add a third rhyming word. See how many rhyming words you and your child can find for one word. You and your child could even make up some silly, nonsense rhyming words like *tope* and *lope* to rhyme with *soap*. This game encourages your child to use her imagination. You can giggle together over "silly" rhyming words you make up. *There's a Wocket in My*

Pocket by Dr. Seuss has many nonsense rhymes you can read to your toddler.

Children love nursery rhymes. Check out a book of Mother Goose nursery rhymes from the library. Your child will love old favorites like: "Jack be nimble. Jack be quick. Jack jump over the candle stick!" or "Hey Diddle, Diddle. The cat and fiddle. The cow jumped over the moon. The little dog laughed to see such fun. And the dish ran away with the spoon!" or "Jack and Jill went up the hill to fetch a pail of water. Jack fell down and broke his crown and Jill came tumbling after!"

13 Games for You and Your Child

Playing is as important for your child's learning as good food is to nourish a growing body. When babies and young children play with a toy or an object, they feel it, smell it, look at it, listen to it and even taste it. This is how young children learn about things. You are also helping to teach your child language when the two of you play together. Sometimes we don't realize a baby is playing because some play looks like naughty behavior. Be tolerant as your baby explores his world. Take time to see the wonder in his eyes. He has a whole, new, amazing world to explore. To him, everything in his world is new and exciting.

Imagine that an 8-month-old has just taken a banana and squished it between her fingers. Imagine that a toddler has just dumped a box full of toys on the floor. These behaviors might seem naughty. How could a child be learning from these behaviors? What could he learn? Actually, the child is learning a lot.

In the first case with the banana, the baby was able to feel a wonderful, new texture. The banana felt cool, soft, creamy and sticky. The banana probably felt like nothing else the child had ever touched. Squishing the banana felt good to the child. Imagine how good that squashed banana felt! Help give your child language about the banana. Try saying, "That banana feels so good. You squeezed the banana, but bananas are for eating, honey. If you want to squeeze, here's a

Hold your baby securely and talk cheerfully as you
introduce baby to a new experience like petting a horse.

clean, wet sponge." Your baby could also squeeze a
yarn ball or a squeezable, empty dishwashing detergent bottle.

Think about the second example with the box and
the dumped toys. Toddlers love to empty things and
dump things out. Dumping out the box of toys might
seem naughty, but dumping the toys teaches things to
your child. The child will slowly learn after dumping
many, many boxes what happens if he turns a box
upside down. Things fall out of a box when the box is
turned over. To grown-ups this seems like a simple
idea, but to a toddler this is a big, new idea. Toddlers
need lots of time and practice to learn ideas like what
happens with dumped boxes. He will also learn what

kinds of sounds certain things make when they fall on the ground. Move any boxes, baskets, or buckets with breakable things out of your toddler's reach. He will dump out whatever he finds. He won't do this to be naughty. He will do it because he is curious. He wants to learn. Let him learn. Give him pots and pans, and clean, empty margarine containers and yogurt cups so he can get lots of practice. Let him discover new ideas about filling and pouring out for himself. Use language to **help** him learn. Try saying, "All of the toys fell out. You turned the box over. You poured out all the toys."

Babies work hard while playing with pots and tubs and learning to pour carefully.

Sound Games

Sound games sharpen your child's listening skills. Play sound games using familiar words your child knows. Ask your child to listen to a word you say and to tell what sound *begins* the word. Your child could also tell you the *ending* sound of a word for another game or the *middle* sounds of words. Here are some easy words many preschool children know:

Starting Sounds	Middle Sounds	Ending Sounds
all	run	lick
doggy	mouse	nyum-nyum
cat	squeak	cup
foo-foo	pool	brush
toy	supper	hand
hat	washing	bell
mama	water	meat
ball	ride	leaf
sock	bed	bus
ice cream	daddy	rain
kitty	light	woof-woof

As your child learns to hear the sounds in simple words, you can begin to use harder words like *hamburger, pencil, and shampoo.* These words have several middle sounds.

Keep in mind that naming sounds in words will be too difficult for toddlers and very young children who are just beginning the wonderful work of learning how words and objects go together, like the word *cup* for the object *cup* that your toddler loves to hold at dinner time.

Parents can do a lot of "dancing" with their children's growing minds. Dancing means that parents keep changing the way they do things with their children as the children learn more and more. For a child learning to hear sounds, the word *stethoscope* would be very hard. It is a long words with many sounds. A child would find the word *soap* much easier to hear sounds when she is just learning. As the child gets better and better at hearing sounds, she can move on to a word that is a little harder like *slippery*. When the child has had *lots* of practice listening to words, she will notice that s*oap*, s*idestep*, and s*tethoscope* all begin and end with the same sound.

Be sure to use easy words at first with your baby. If a child is given a very hard word as she is first learning, she might not be able to play word-naming games. She might give up because the game was too hard. Building up, or "dancing" your way up, to a hard word makes the game better and more fun for the child. As you *slowly* make the games harder, you are tuning into your child. You are keeping pace with your child's learning. Sometimes a child needs you to go slowly in making a learning game harder. Sometimes he will enjoy it when you challenge him with a slightly harder game. You know your child best! Be a good "matchmaker." Match how hard your language games are to your child's level of comfort. The secret is to keep your child challenged *and* feeling successful. Games shouldn't be too hard or too easy.

Try saying a word and ask your child to say a word that begins with the same sound. You could also change the game by asking your child to say a word that ends with the same sound. Be very accepting of your child's answers. Imagine your child is trying to think of a word that starts with the sound *t* and says "stop." Instead of saying "You're wrong," help your child to hear the right sound. Try saying, "Let's say that word together. Stop. *S S S s*top. What sound is that? The word stop does have a *t* sound, but what is the first sound you hear? Right! You heard an *s* sound first! Good for you! You are a good listener!" If you let your child know it's OK to make mistakes, she will grow up willing to try to learn new things. Learning is often a hard struggle. *Making mistakes and keeping on trying are big steps in learning.*

If your child is having trouble thinking of a word, give him a hint. Point to an object that begins with the sound you said. If your child is trying to think of a *p* word, point to a piece of paper or a pan. You are dancing down and making the learning game easier for your child.

The games in this chapter help your child learn to listen and to hear and to learn the many sounds in our language. Your child will learn how different sounds are put together to make different words. Be sure to say beginning, middle, and ending sounds in words when you are talking to your child. If your child can hear the beginning, middle, and ending sounds of words, spelling words will be easier for him later in school. He needs to hears all of the sounds in a word so he can spell the word. To give you an example of how important it is to speak clearly to your child and say all the sounds, here is the story of a child who thought that a chest of drawers was a piece of furniture named after someone called Chester Drawers. She never heard that *three* words, *chest of drawers* were being said. It sounded like one long word, *Chesterdrawers.* The chant "Pat-a-cake, pat-a-cake" is often heard by children as "paddy cake, paddy cake."

14 Games To Give Your Child a Strong Body and a Strong Mind

Some days your child may seem to have too much energy. Maybe you've done everything you can think of to entertain your child like reading stories and making cookies and he still has too much energy. Maybe he just wants to run around your house! Body games are great for days like this because your child can use all his energy by moving his legs, and arms, and head. Body games will help your child to stretch and use his muscles to have a strong body. The language you use while you're playing the game with your child will help him have a strong mind! Here are some great body games to play with your child.

Hooray for Me!

Have your child kneel in a little ball on the floor. Have your child slowly curl upward over her knees, over her hips, over her stomach, up to her shoulders. Have her stretch her arms and head up high and jump up high as she shouts, "Hooray for Me!" Try putting words with this game, too. You and your child can play this game while pretending to be elevators. As you slowly curl upward say, "I'm an elevator going up, up, up, up . . . Hooray for Me!" Let your voice get

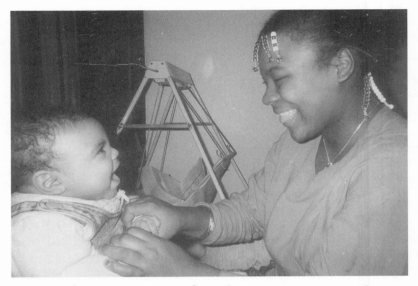

Have fun as you pretend to play see-saw on your lap.

louder and louder as you say "up, up, up, up" and shout "Hooray for Me!" or let your voice get softer and softer until you are whispering.

Roll the Ball!

The idea of this game is to use lots of language while you and your child roll or toss a ball back and forth to each other. Use a large, soft, rubber ball. A large ball will be easier for your small child to catch. You want to use a soft, rubber ball because a hard ball can hurt a small child if the ball is thrown a little too hard. For a young child, roll the ball instead of tossing the ball. Catching a ball in the air is too hard for many toddlers. Say, "I'm rolling the ball to you. Daddy is rolling the ball to Maria. You caught the ball! Now

Babies love to roll a ball back and forth with you.

roll the ball back to Daddy. Maria is rolling the ball to Daddy!"

Playground Fun!

A playground is a wonderful place to spend some time with your child. The equipment and toys on a playground are special for making your child's body stronger. The talking you do with your child on the playground will teach him more about using language. Spend some time running and stretching in an open, grassy area of the playground. Teach your child how to pump his legs on a swing to make himself go. Help your child go down the slide. If your young child doesn't feel ready to go on a big slide, try using a smaller slide. Say, "You're climbing up the ladder. Climbing to the top. Now you're at the top of the slide. You're sitting at the top of the slide. Down you go! Sliding down, down, down to the ground! You did it!"

15 Easy Toys You Can Make from Things at Home

You don't have to have fancy, store-bought toys for your child to have fun. You have the makings for some terrific toys right in your home!

Water Play

Children love to explore with water. Children learn best when they can "do" things with materials. They like "hands on" games. This way, they can be scientists. They can figure out what happens *if* they do this or that. Waterplay is a great learning activity. All you need is a sink, or a basin, or your bathtub. You could also use some empty cans, orange juice cans, or big and little plastic cups. If you have other materials like a colander, a funnel, drinking straws, corks, or spoons, add them too.

Your child will love *pouring* water from a cup to a can. Try poking a small hole in the bottom of a can. Your child will learn what *drip* means. Have your child look at the amount of water big and little cups can hold. Which has *more?* Which has *less?* Your child can discover what kinds of things *float* and *sink*. Talk with your child about how the water feels. Is it *wet* or *dry? Cold* or *warm?* Just think of the new words you and your child can talk about together: *drip, pouring fast, pouring slow, more, less, sink, float, wet, dry, cold, warm, sprinkle.*

Your child will need time to play without talking or answering your questions. Give your child time to play and discover on her own. Then you can talk about what she has discovered.

To cut down on the messiness of water play, put newspaper under the water tub. Remember that water is messy, and your child will spill some, so set up the water in a safe area. If you don't want water play in your house, try playing outside with a plastic dish tub in warm weather. Bathtime or laundry time are other good times for waterplay. If your child is playing in the bathtub, make sure the water is shallow—only a few inches of water.

Always stay with your child when she is playing with water. Even a small amount of water (as little as three or four inches) can be dangerous for your young child. Toddlers easily lose their balance when they are splashing in the tub. If a young child falls and her face lands in the water, she may not be able to think to move her face out of the water. Thinking and planning how to do things and how to make things happen are *very hard* for children. If the phone rings or someone comes to the door, take your child out of the water or move the water tub out of her reach. *Never* leave your child alone with water, not even for a few minutes.

The Egg Carton Color Game

This is a great game that teaches your child about colors and sorting things into colors. You need a few sheets of colored paper, a bowl, a white Styrofoam egg carton, and some magic markers. If you don't have colored paper, your toddler can color sheets of white paper with different color crayons. This is a fun job for your child.

Ask your child to pick out a color crayon or a magic marker. Ask him to name the color. Naming the color of a marker each time he uses a new marker color will help him learn his colors. Have your child color the inside of one of the egg carton cups. Each cup in the egg carton will be a different color.

After the cups in the egg carton have been colored, ask your child to tear each sheet of colored paper into strips. Then he can tear the strips of paper into small pieces. Tearing pieces of paper gives your child lots of practice in using the small muscles in her hands and fingers! Mix all of the colored paper pieces together in a bowl.

Next, ask your child to pick out a piece of colored paper from the bowl. Have your child tell you the color of each piece of paper. Point to the egg carton and say, "Which cup does that piece of paper go to? What color does it match in the egg carton? Show me where the paper goes." The game goes on until each egg carton cup is filled with paper pieces that are the same color as the cup.

If your child is just beginning to learn her colors, use only two or three colors in this game like red, green, and yellow. Be sure you name each color several times during the game. Hearing you say each color and point to each color will help your child learn her colors.

If the child is really sure of himself at this game, sometimes try a trick. Your child might pick up a bit of red paper. You could then ask, "That goes in the yellow egg cup, doesn't it?" Your child will enjoy catching you making a mistake. Your child will enjoy playing "teacher" and telling you the right answer.

When your child has learned easy color names, then teach him more colors. Some more difficult colors are: turquoise (blue-green), rose, violet, tan, and gray. As your child learns these harder color names, say "You sure are learning the names for many different colors. I am really proud of how many colors you are learning."

The Color Mixing Game

This game gives children a chance to experiment with mixing colors and creating new colors. For this game you need plastic bowls, food coloring, and some spoons. In order to make a new color out of two colors, you have to start with *primary* colors. In a package of food coloring, the primary colors are *red, yellow,* and *blue.*

Help your child fill five bowls about half-full of water and put them on the floor or on a table. Next, ask your child to squeeze two drops of red coloring in one bowl, two drops of yellow in one bowl, and two drops of blue in one bowl. Ask your child to name the colors as he adds a different color to each bowl of water. Leave the other two bowls filled with plain water.

Put a spoon beside each bowl to use in mixing colors. Let your child experiment with mixing different colors together in the plain water. Red and yellow will make orange. Yellow and blue will make green. When your child creates a new color, ask your child how she did it. Say, "How did you make some orange water? You put a spoonful of red water and a spoonful of yellow water in the bowl and mixed the red and yellow together. Red and yellow mixed together make orange." Talking about what she did will give her practice using language, and it will help her understand how she made a new color. Your young child won't understand about mixing colors to make new colors, but he will enjoy pouring the colored water into the different bowls.

A toddler who uses the spoon to scoop up water and then pours the water from the spoon into the bowl gets good practice in controlling hand movements. Squeezing the food coloring bottles give good practice for the small muscles in little hands.

The Feely Box Game

This is a guessing game for using language. For this game you need a box with a top, like a shoebox and some familiar, household objects. Make a hole in the box top big enough for your child's hand to fit through and feel objects. Fill the box with objects that the child knows really well. Here are some objects you might use:

- a small piece of towel or terrycloth
- a thick piece of yarn
- a cotton ball
- an empty juice can
- some plastic milk carton tops
- a shoe lace
- a small sponge
- a yogurt cup
- a brush
- a comb
- a very large button
- a small pencil with a dull end
- a small rock
- a toothbrush
- a piece of soap
- a piece of sandpaper

Have your child reach into the Feely Box. Tell her not to look, just feel. Ask her to talk about what she feels. Ask her to guess what the object is. Ask her, "How can you tell? What do you feel that helps you guess what you're holding?"

Sometimes a baby needs you to steady her birthday present so she can open it herself.

Let your child take the object out of the box. Was her guess correct? If she named the item correctly, then she can leave this item out. If she didn't guess correctly, put the item back in the box. Guessing correctly will be easier for her the next time.

Teach your child words to describe how *hard* the rock feels or how *scratchy* the sandpaper feels. Talk about how *bristly* a brush feels or how smooth the button feels. Use shape words like the *round* button and the *square* sponge.

The game is over when all the objects have been taken out of the box. Praise your child for using shape words and for using words to describe how the objects felt. Praise your child for being a good *detective*. Your child is learning to *feel* clues with his hands. He learns to *see* with his eyes. He learns to *tell* with his mouth.

Making Playdough

Playdough is a well-loved activity for children. Make your own playdough at home with your child. Here is the recipe:

3 cups flour

1½ cups salt

¼ cup vegetable oil

1 cup water

3 drops of any color food coloring [add to the water]

This playdough does not have to be cooked. Mix all of the ingredients in a large bowl by hand with a big spoon. You and your child can measure each ingredient together before you pour the ingredient into the bowl. Count out three cups of flour, for instance. As your child mixes the ingredients, talk about the changes in the way the ingredients look. For example, what happens to the flour when you add the water? The flour was *dry*. Now it is *wet*. It looks different. Ask your child to use words to describe what he sees happening.

A large plastic glass, a rolling pin or a soda bottle can be used to roll out the playdough. As your child is rolling out the playdough, say, "You're rolling out the playdough. You're pushing down on the rolling pin (or bottle) and pushing out. You're making the play-dough flatter, and flatter." If you have any old cookie cutters, bring them out to use with the playdough. Try using plastic forks, spatulas, or bottle caps to make prints in the playdough. The playdough will last for about two weeks in a tightly sealed container.

Empty and Fill Games

Older infants and toddlers love to pour things out and fill things up. Picking up things and putting them into a container is just the right practice for little

Your pots and pans make
wonderful toys for babies to explore.

hands that need to develop more control in not spilling juice. Try gathering some objects like a coffee can, a plastic pitcher or water bottle. If you can find a bottle that is skinnier at the top that's even better. If you use a coffee can, cut a hole (just slightly bigger than the objects your child is picking up) in the top of the lid.

For one game, fill a container with wooden clothespins. Find the kind that doesn't pinch. Your toddler will love dumping the clothespins out and then putting them back in the container.

Try using other materials like popsicle sticks you've saved. If you use popsicle sticks, try cutting slits in the plastic top of a coffee can so your toddler can *push* the smooth sticks *through* the slit *into* the can.

Talk about puzzle pieces and where they go
as you work together on the floor.

You could use wooden blocks, large bristle blocks, or large Lego pieces. If you have an older child, you may already have some of these toys. Check around at garage sales for toys, too. Make sure you wash the toys you use. *Make sure the toys are too big to fit in your child's mouth.* Small toys can be swallowed and cause choking.

Treasures at the Dollar Store

Look around at a dollar store or variety store in your area for goodies. Sometimes you can find cookie cutter sets, low-priced puzzles, paints, markers, balls, books, and different kinds of plastic bottles and cups. If you look carefully, you may be able to find some good materials for your home-made games.

16 A Sense of Humor with Funny Jokes and Silly Words

Older toddlers and young children are beginning to develop a sense of humor. You can help your toddler's sense of humor grow. Suppose your toddler puts her foot in a coffee can, grins at you and says, "Mama, shoe!" This is a good sign that your baby is starting to develop a sense of humor. She knows the coffee can isn't a shoe. She's making a joke!

Jokes with Your Young Baby

You can even help your young baby grow a sense of humor. People who study babies tell us that babies like jokes they can *feel* and *hear* when they are 4–6 months old. Crawling babies sometimes like their mamas or papas to tickle them gently and say, "I'm gonna get you!" in a playful voice. Be sure to watch your baby's face. Sometimes a game that starts out feeling happy turns scary for a baby. Keep the game going *only* while your baby feels happy about it.

Babies also like to hear funny, big sounds like "foo-foo" or "physicist." When you say those words, make them sound funny. Say the *f* in "foo-foo" in a big way.

Babies 7–9 months old like to *see* funny things.

95

Babies love giggling and special attention
from their family.

Your baby might thinks it's so funny to see his papa
shaking a cloth in his mouth like a puppy or walking
like a duck who waddles from side to side.

Older infants and toddlers like to make things happen as a funny joke. Young children think jack-in-the-
box toys are so funny. Toddlers love jack-in-the-box
toys because *they can make* the funny clown jump up.
Toddlers like to do things for themselves! They enjoy
feeling in charge of the funny pop-up toy.

Funny, Silly Songs

Toddlers love to hear silly songs and to think about
things that don't go together. For example, most

young children love the song "The Bear Went Over the Mountain." You can change this song to make it silly. You can sing: "The bear went over the mountain, the bear went over the mountain, the bear went over the mountain to see what he could see. And all that he could see and all that he could see, and all that he could see was a goat in a boat." Other silly verses might be a skunk on a trunk, a snake in a cake, or a cat in a hat.

Another silly song is called "Down by the Bay." Here are the words: "Down by the bay, where the watermelons grow, back to my home, I dare not go. For if I do, my mother will say, did you ever see a goose kissing a moose, down by the bay" [repeat with another silly verse.] Other silly verses might be whale with a polk-a-dot tail, a fly wearing a tie, or a llama wearing some pajamas. You and your child can make up many more verses.

If you are singing a silly song with an older child, your toddler may not understand the words but she'll enjoy the rhymes. She will giggle along with you and your older child.

"Knock-Knock" Jokes and Funny Words

Many young children love telling "Knock-Knock" jokes. Often, they don't quite understand what the joke is. Young children don't always have enough understanding of language to recognize the play on words that is a part of "knock-knock" jokes. They may say, "Knock-knock. Who's there? Apple. Apple who? Eat an apple," and then laugh hysterically. Sometimes they don't even say the last line ("Eat an apple"). They may just look at you and wait for you to laugh. Be supportive of their attempts at trying to make jokes. You might say, "I like for you to tell me jokes!"

Sometimes a developing sense of humor can be very silly. One group of preschoolers was making vegetable stew with their teacher. They began talking about all of the different kinds of soup like chicken noodle, vegetable, and tomato soup. Suddenly one child said "banana soup," and he burst out laughing. The group of children all began laughing and saying silly soup names like banana soupee, hamburger soupee, and spoon soupee.

Tickle your little one as long as baby looks happy.

If a young child starts saying silly things like hamburger soupee or spoon soupee, it might seem like he's trying to be sassy. He isn't trying to be smart or sassy. He really is just making a joke!

Even though these games seem silly to us as adults, they are very important to children. For one thing, children are using language. Singing silly songs, for example, often make children want to talk and point out the impossibility of what you've said. If you are singing about a whale wearing a polk-a-dot tail, your child may take delight in telling you "Whales don't wear ties, you silly Mama!" Experts tell us that humor is important to the development of a creative, smart brain.

17 Imagination and Your Child

Many young children have wild imaginations. They like to *pretend*. Pretend games are things children make up in their minds. For instance, a child playing in the mud might pretend to make a delicious chocolate cake for his daddy. Pretending is a wonderful way to make games more fun. Pretending is also great for sharpening a child's mind. Sometimes children like to pretend they are different people. Your child might pretend to be you because he really loves you. He might try to copy things you do at home. He might try to walk like you do or talk like you do. Children sometimes pretend to be superheroes like Batman.

Pretend Friends and Made-Up Stories

Children often have pretend friends. One mother reported that one day as she was fixing lunch, her three-year-old pointed to an empty chair at the table and asked for a sandwich for her friend "George." George was an imaginary friend, a friend this child made up in her mind.

If your child tells you stories about pretend people, you might think that your child is lying to you. This isn't true. Having an imagination is a good thing. It means that your child is smart and creative.

Encourage your child to be creative. You can have

Kids can create their own playful shadow pictures
when the sun is out.

pretend lunches and teas for you, your child, and your
child's imaginary friend. There are lots of chances for
language and conversation here. Ask your child questions about her "friend." Try to get her to think creatively about her "friend." You might say to your
child, "Tell me some things about your friend" or
"What are your friend's favorite foods?" or "What are
your friend's favorite games to play?" These kinds of
comments leave lots of room for your child to tell you
anything she wants about her friend. These comments
are called open-ended because there is no one right
or wrong answer. You could also ask about what toys

the imaginary friend likes to play with, where she lives, or what she's doing right now.

Some imagination games can go on for years! A mother and father told the story of an imagination game they played with their young children for several years. When their twin daughters were two-and-a-half or three-years old, they began talking about fairies. This idea probably came from a story. The children reported that fairies lived in the house. The parents encouraged this imagination game by asking the children questions. Where did the fairies live? What did they eat? What do they look like? How do they talk?

Seeing that their parents were interested in their stories, the children answered all the questions and thought of a lot of details about the fairies. The parents even left notes at night "from the fairies." The fairies would thank the children for letting them live in the house and for making pictures for them and other things. Sometimes the parents and children went on fairy hunts and looked for fairy footprints! It was a creative adventure for everyone involved.

When You Think Your Child Is Fibbing

Sometimes children make up stories about other children at school or about people they know. Remember that your child isn't trying to lie. Young children have a hard time understanding what is real and what isn't real. As they get older, they will learn how to tell the difference between fantasy and reality. While they're young, though, you might have to help. Be supportive when your child tells you a story. If the child tells you a serious story about her being hurt or scared, don't ignore her. Gently ask your child questions about the story. Try to find out if the story has any truth in it. Try to find out why your child told you the story. Maybe she is worried about something and wanted to get your attention. In other words, there might be some reason for her story. Finding out that your child completely made up a story may make you angry. You may feel less annoyed if you know that very young children really don't have the skills to be sneaky and make up a story to lie to you on purpose.

Imagination-Building Games

One thing you can do to help your child's imagination to grow is to give her opportunities to *use* her imagination. Many of the toys you can buy for three-and-four-year-olds are prepackaged and ready-to-go. The child takes the toy out. She plays with it, and then she puts it away. She doesn't always need to use a lot of brain power. Children need to stretch their pretending skills just as they need to stretch their muscles.

Magic Made-Up Stories

Making up pretend stories is a good way for your child to stretch his pretending skills. Gather some old door keys or car keys and put them in a box. With your child, pick out a key. Ask your child, "Who can use a key like this? What will it unlock?" Act very interested in your child's answers. Encourage her to make up stories about what she can explore with the keys.

Another idea is to put objects like small rocks or some macaroni into an empty juice can. Cover the end of the can with the plastic lid. Tell your child, "I have a treasure in here. Listen to the noise it makes. [Shake the can.] What could it be? Where did it come from? Tell me a story about this treasure." Use a "mystery" voice. Ask these questions slowly. You want to give your child time to think about what could be in the can. Even if she doesn't correctly guess what is in the can, appreciate your child's interesting answer!

The Magic Sheet Game

Believe it or not, an ordinary white bedsheet can make a wonderful imagination game for your child! With the Magic Sheet Game your child can "play in the snow" in the middle of the summer! Here's how: spread the sheet on the floor. Help your child pretend to make snow angels by lying down on the sheet and flapping his arms and legs.

Sit on the "snow" (the white sheet) and pretend to build a snowman. Pretend to roll a gigantic ball of snow. Say, "Let's roll the snow [roll the pretend ball around the sheet]." Pretend the snow is really cold. Then pretend to roll another ball and say, "Now let's lift up the snowball and put it on top of the first snowball we made. This is the snowman's middle. Oh, it's very heavy!" Once the snowman is built, pretend to decorate him with imaginary clothing like a hat, a scarf, and so on. This may sound like a silly game, but children have wonderful imaginations! You can help your child's imagination grow with games like the Magic Sheet!

Use your magic sheet as a pretend swimming pool. Your child can lie on her stomach and show you how she kicks as she swims. She can move her arms as if she were swimming. You and your child can pretend to splash water on each other.

Pretend the magic sheet is a boat and the floor around the sheet is the ocean or the lake. Pretend to steer the boat. Pretend to use oars to row so the boat will move through the water. Ask your child what he sees as the two of you are sailing. Does he see other boats? Storm clouds approaching? An island with a buried treasure? Whales or fish? Birds flying in the sky? Show your child how to make binoculars or a telescope by making your hands into circles, holding them up to your eyes and looking through the circles. Explain to your child that binoculars and telescopes help you see things that are far away. Pretend to fish from your boat or jump in the water to take a swim [have your child pretend to put on a life-jacket or life preserver, since children should always swim with an adult and should always wear a life-jacket].

The Imagination House

Another great imagination game that makes children think and use their imaginations has been around for years. The next time your child is playing house, let her build a house out of a bedsheet draped across chairs. Children get really creative with this game. Some children think of adding pillows and boxes for windows or furniture. Sheets can be tied back in some places to make doors.

This is a game that young children can play for hours, and you don't have to buy anything to play it. The game is also important because it helps your child learn to think creatively and then to talk about her ideas. If several children from your neighborhood are playing together, they can learn to get along with each other, to cooperate in playing this game.

The Magic Knick-Knack Game

Another imagination game involves household objects or knick-knacks around the house. Children can think of imaginative ways to use something familiar.

For example, they might suggest that an empty, round oatmeal box with a lid on could be a drum or a rolling toy or a chef's hat on the head when the box is worn upside down without the top on. Choose some toys and objects your child knows well. Here are some ideas for toys and objects to use:

- a large paper bag
- a large square of cloth
- a bouncy ball
- a box with a top
- a clean, empty plastic detergent bottle
- wooden spoons
- clean, empty yogurt cups
- a long piece of yarn
- clean, empty milk cartons

Pick out an object, like the box with a lid. Tell your child, "A person can do lots of things with a box." You could ask, "What are some things you have seen Mr. Box do?" Your child may answer, "Carry things." Then say, "You're right. Boxes are used to carry things. Now let's try to think of lots of ways to use Mr. Box. Let's think hard. As soon as you think of a new way to use Mr. Box, you tell me!"

Ask questions like this for each item. As your child gives ideas, praise him. Say, "That is a good thing you could do with Mr. Box. Now tell me another thing. Think of another way you could use the box."

Give your child lots of time to think about each object. Don't pick a new object right away. Give your child a chance to use his imagination. Make sure you give your child lots of praise and encouragement for his creative ideas!

You could also make a list of all of the ideas you and your child have told each other. Anytime you can bring writing into a game, you are teaching your child

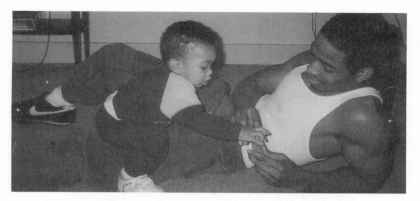

Help your baby pretend: Could a grey rock be a chair?
Could it be a little mouse that goes "squeak, squeak"?

about writing and that writing has a purpose. Remember that using language by *talking* and *writing* will help children later on to learn to read and to do better in school.

Art Activities for Babies and Toddlers

Babies and toddlers will love art experiences like fingerpainting using instant pudding. Imagine how interesting the creamy, smooth pudding will feel to your baby as she spreads the pudding on paper or a table top. Using instant pudding for paint is a safe and delicious way for babies and toddlers to paint! Make sure to take time to talk about how pudding paint feels, looks, and tastes!

Playing with soft, squishy playdough will be another favorite with your toddler. Homemade playdough is easy to make with flour, salt, water, and cream of tartar. The salty playdough won't taste very good but it won't hurt your toddler if she decides to take a bite.

Your baby will love to fingerpaint
with instant chocolate pudding.

Another activitiy idea is to let your older baby or
toddler place balls of fluffy cotton, pieces of brightly
colored paper, and pieces of material on a piece of
sticky, clear contact paper. Feeling the contact paper
will be a great touching experience, and it is a way to
make a collage without glue.

Toddlers and young children will enjoy using
chalk and chalkboards as they experiment with making their first pictures. Also try giving your toddler or
young child big, washable markers and a large piece
of paper. Crayons may be too difficult for babies who
might want to chew on them.

18 Does TV Help Your Child's Language Grow?

Television is a big part of most families' lives. That means that children watch a lot of television. Sometimes a mama or a daddy might leave a TV on for the company. Sometimes it's nice to hear the voices on TV if you are home alone with your child on a rainy, dark day.

Is TV good or bad for your child's learning? We'll tell you some not-so-good things about television and some good news about the TV. Watching television can be OK for a child. The key is *how much* television a child watches and *what kinds* of programs the child watches.

The Bad News about TV

In our country, children watch a lot of TV, sometimes up to four or five hours a day. Scientists who study about children and television, tell us that watching too much television is bad for children because they don't develop certain skills they need. For example, watching TV doesn't give children much opportunity to use their brains. TV program material moves very quickly. Young children have to *learn how to think* and *how to take information* and *store it in their brains.* When the programs move so quickly, it is hard for children to think that fast and to store information in their brain so quickly. If they watch a lot of television, they may have a hard time learning these skills. This means that young children who watch hours of television may have problems a few years later in school when they have to *read* something and *talk* about it or *write* about it.

Part of the problem is that language used on television is spoken very quickly and it isn't always grammatically correct. Think of the chapter in this book that talked about how important it is for your child to hear clearly the words you say. The same thing is true for television. Notice that people on TV often talk too fast. Children can't catch all the words in sentences and the way words should be put together in language. Second, children need to hear people on TV say sentences with all the right parts in order: the nouns, verbs, adjectives, adverbs, pronouns, and prepositions. If children never hear the right way a sentence is supposed to be put together, then they will have trouble in school later when they must write a correct sentence or read and understand a correct sentence in a school textbook.

Experts tell us that most TV shows are so fast-paced that children have a hard time following the plot or storyline. The term *pace* means how fast the scene or picture changes on the TV screen. Did you know that most commercials have scenes that are only on your TV screen for about 2 seconds?

Studies tell us that children who watch very fast-paced programs (which are usually prime-time shows) have problems paying attention to their work and to teachers in school. They are distracted very easily.

The Good News about TV

The good news is that there are some shows on TV that are better for your child than others. It is also very important that you watch TV *with* your child. Experts tell us that when children watch educational shows like *Sesame Street* and *Mr. Rogers Neighborhood* with their parents, they learn more from the TV show. When you are there to explain things on TV to your child and to answer your child's questions, TV becomes a much more positive influence.

Often, your young child may watch a TV show that has complicated language. Young children have a very limited understanding of the structure of language. They don't understand that words in a sentence can be switched around, or that there are different ways of talking. Even shows like *Sesame Street* can sometimes have confusing language for children. You can help by explaining things on TV to your child. If a conversation on TV seems kind of long and detailed to you, ask your child, "Do you understand what they're talking about?" If the answer is no, take a moment to explain.

When you are watching TV together, help your child *learn to listen.* Listening is a skill that has to be learned. After a few lines of talking on TV ask your child, "What are they talking about?" You may want to focus your child's attention on what is going on, why people or puppets are acting the way they do. Help your child remember what they are talking about on the TV program. Talk with your child about what she heard.

Your child can have a more active part in watching TV by *thinking* about what is happening and *thinking* about the plot of the TV show. After the TV show, ask your child to tell you something he remembers from the show. This will make him think and recall what he watched. Older children can retell the TV show in their own words. Children must be able to understand language and to *use* it well in order to succeed in school.

How To Make Watching TV Better for Your Child

First of all, try to limit the amount of TV your child watches everyday. Many parents like to use TV as a babysitter. They figure that when their children watch TV, the children will calm down and be quiet, especially when a favorite TV show is playing. If your children can grow up with a love for books, then they will be able to calm down by reading or looking at a book instead of TV. Try to think of other activities besides TV that can keep your child busy when you are busy. Here are some other things your child can do:

- Give your child some books to look at or read.
- Let your child play with home-made playdough.
- Let your child play with the games and toys you've made from empty containers.
- Check out a tape-recorder and some children's music tapes from the public library and let your child listen to some music. *Peter and the Wolf* is a great classic where each musical instrument represents a different character in the story: Peter, the duck, the bird, the grandfather, and, of course, the wolf!
- Give your child crayons and paper and ask her make a picture for the refrigerator or wall. Tell him to be thinking of a special place you can hang his picture. Make a big deal about hanging it up. You can save paper grocery bags to

use as coloring paper. Paper bags are also good for your child to cut on with safe, child-size scissors. Cutting is a good skill she'll need to learn for school.

• Encourage your child to play imaginary games. Build a "house" out of a bedsheet draped over a chair.

• Save clean, empty, half-gallon milk cartons to make safe building blocks for your child. Put two milk cartons together by sliding one carton inside the other. [The open end of one carton slides into the open end of the other carton.] You can cover the carton blocks with contact paper, leave them plain, or let your child color on his new "blocks" with magic markers.

When your child does watch TV, try to watch the show with your child. Be *picky* about the shows you and your child watch. We know from science studies that children who watch a lot of TV, especially fast-paced, violent shows, have a harder time learning to read. They have lower reading levels in school. Children who watch a lot of violent TV programs don't seem to have as much imagination as other children.

Children who watch too many violent TV shows don't seem to care as much if others get hurt. Violence teaches children a dangerous lesson. It teaches them that the way to solve problems in getting along with others is to try to hurt or destroy others.

Make a special effort to watch educational shows like *Sesame Street, Mr. Rogers' Neighborhood,* and *Barney.* The public television channel (PBS) often has special shows for children. Remember that your child's brain needs exercise just as her muscles do.

19 Good Things To Do With Your Baby When You're Not at Home

Children learn by seeing new things and going new places. Being with you outside of your home helps your child learn. Whenever you can, take your child with you to the grocery store, to the library, to the laundromat, to the park, or just for a walk in the fresh air. Also, take a trip to a playground with baby and toddler size equipment, such as low climbers.

An Adventure in Your Community

Even walking around your block you will notice lots of chances to help your child learn. Look at letters on signs. A stop sign begins with the letter S. Find all of the stop signs and the S's along your path. Other signs might be "One Way," "No Parking," and the "Bus Stop" sign. Help your child find a letter in her name.

Count how many *red* cars you see (or any color). *Count* the number of houses on a block. *Count* the cracks in the sidewalk. *Count* the number of bicycles you and your child see in yards. *Count* the number of people you and your child pass by as you walk.

Feel the sidewalk cement, the bark of a tree, the grass, and the bushes you pass by. Encourage your

114

Toddlers love low climbing bars in a park.

child to talk about how things look and how things feel. The cement feels *hard, rough,* and *warm* from the sun. The bark feels *bumpy.* The grass feels *soft* and *tickly.*

As you walk through the neighborhood or park, talk about the things that you see. Look for people walking their dogs, or comment on other families with their children. Sometimes you see really interesting sights like someone flying a kite in the wind, or someone holding balloons wiggling in the wind.

When you take special trips to the zoo or a county fair, your child can enjoy gently petting baby animals, such as chickens or ponies.

Family time at the park is a special time for toddlers.

Special Events in Town

Most communities have special free events that would make wonderful outings for you and your child. Your daily newspaper, radio, and the local library have listings of special events during the year. Check to see if your community has a science museum for children. In such a museum, children have a chance to handle science experiments and materials. Your community may also have farmers' markets in the fall or spring. Check to see if there are special seasonal festivals like apple-picking time in the fall or a Halloween hayride or a sleigh-ride for children in a community park.

Be Prepared for Stops and Waits

Keep in mind that children get tired very easily. You will need to stop and rest if you have a long walk planned. If you know you will be out for several hours, bring along a sandwich, fruit or juice, and crackers for your child. If you're going to do some grocery shopping, give your child a nutritious snack like apple slices to eat while you shop. Keep him happy while you're busy.

Anytime you take your child to the doctor, you usually end up waiting. Bring along a book, a favorite toy, or some paper and crayons. Some waiting rooms have toys for children, but you will feel much calmer if you come prepared. If there is a window in the waiting room or examination room, your child will enjoy watching and looking for people, cars, buses, trees, and so on. You can pass the time by doing other things like counting how many other children are in the waiting room. Keep in mind that a sick child is extra cranky so be extra-understanding and loving if your child just wants to cry or suck a thumb and cuddle on your lap. Remember how awful it feels to be sick. The doctor's office can sometimes feel like a scary place.

If you are using the city bus to go on an errand, you may have to do some waiting. Sometimes in a laundromat you need to wait a long while. Bring along a favorite book for the wait. Use waiting time to sing rhymes, chants, and songs that you read about in chapter 12. While you and your child are waiting, talk about what you have done together that day. Ask your child to recall the first thing you did today or something you bought at the grocery store or how much fun you had on a picnic last weekend. These are good talking games and good memory games for your child. Use words to keep your child busy. Your genuine, interested conversation will help keep your child from becoming too cranky after a long day and a long wait.

Take Your Baby To Visit Relatives

Babies need special people like family members. They will love being admired and cuddled by close friends and relatives. If your baby is familiar with certain relatives, your visit can become a special event for your child as well as a chance for you to have adult company.

20 When Babytalk and Baby Play Embarrass You

When you use babytalk or play with your baby in front of other people, sometimes you might feel silly. You might think, "People are looking at me." This is a perfectly normal way to feel.

Remember, though, that lots of people talk differently to their babies than to other people. Also remember that people like to look at babies. Many people are very curious about babies. If people are looking at you as you walk through the mall, they are probably looking at and admiring your baby, not listening to what you say. If they do listen to your babytalk with baby, they're probably thinking, "Wow, that baby really likes what he's doing. That father must know a lot about babies. His baby is lucky to have a papa (or mama) who *knows* what babies like!"

You want the best for your baby, and you know that babies enjoy the sounds of babytalk. Feel proud of yourself for doing the right kinds of talking and loving with your baby. You can be a teacher for other parents. If you are sitting at the bus stop with your child playing a game together, or talking or singing songs, other parents are going to be impressed with what a great relationship you have with your child. They may go home and try some of the things with their child that they saw *you* do with your child!

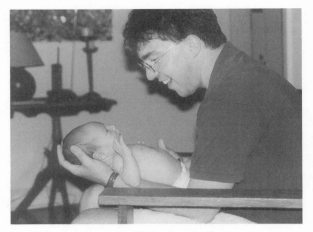

Lots of turn-taking talk helps babies grow smart.

Whether tiny or growing bigger, babies will look right
into your eyes when you talk lovingly to them.

The bottom line is do what you know is right, and don't worry about what other people think. *You're* the one who has been reading about *how* to start from early babyhood to make your child *smarter* before school and happier too!

21 What You Can Say When Your Child Says Words You Don't Want To Hear

Almost every child says a naughty word at one point or another. Remember to be careful of what you say at home. Children will say what they hear their parents say. Children may also pick up bad words from other children in the neighborhood or at childcare.

When children say bad words, *they don't know what the words mean.* They only know that this is what people say when they are mad or frustrated. Sometimes a child will shout out a bad word to get attention. Young children don't know what the word means. But they sure do know that they will get a big reaction out of somebody if they say it.

When your child says words you don't want to hear, be firm but positive with your child. Explain to your child that this is not a word that is OK to say. You might say something like, "Devon, that's an ugly word. It can hurt people's feelings. I know you heard someone say it, but I don't want you to say it again." If your child is angry when he says the word, try saying, "I know you're mad. I need you to think of another word to say, though. That word is not OK to say. If you're mad, you can say *"I'm so mad!"* Perhaps your child could make up his own "mad word" like "Grump-ti-dump!"

Sometimes you can help your child to get her anger out by giving her some playdough to pound and roll. When she's angry she can really pound the playdough!

Your child may say a bad word even when he doesn't seem angry. He may say the word to get your attention or get some kind of a reaction out of you. Make your reaction small so that you don't encourage him to use the word again. If you make a big deal out of it, you've given him a lot of attention, and he'll do it again.

The first time your child says a bad word explain that saying the word is not OK for you. The next time she says the word, say calmly but firmly, "I'm not going to listen to that word. When you get ready to use your own words, I'd love to talk to you. I'll be in the kitchen when your ready." Then leave the room and go into the kitchen. Being in a different room gives you a better chance to stay in control, and you haven't become mad or yelled at your child.

If your child is saying the word as an attention-getter, try to spend more time with him during the day. If you give him more of your time and do something special with him, he won't need to say the attention word.

Another technique to try if your child absolutely needs to say unacceptable words is to tell him to go in a private place, like the bathroom, and say that word over and over until he feels he has said it enough. Then he can come out and be where you are.

22 How To Get Your Child To Do What You Want Without Getting Mad

Being a parent is a really hard job. Sometimes you get so frustrated, you just want to scream. Remembering that your child *is just a child* can help you stay in control.

Your child has only been on this earth a short time. She really doesn't know the right way to act or what to do. She can't always act "like a big girl" because she *doesn't know how*. Part of your job as a parent is to *teach* your child appropriate ways to act. Try to be patient.

Many times your child needs to know that *you* know how *he* feels. Try to understand how your child feels and thinks about things. Do a lot of talking when you're trying to get your child to do something. Help your child understand *why* he has to do something. No one likes to take orders from a bigger person, not even children.

Imagine that you are trying to get your child to pick up her toys. You could say, "Put that up right now! Do it, NOW!" but is that the *best* way? You feel awful for yelling at your child, and your child feels sad and mad if you're yelling at her. Try saying, "I know it is hard to pick up your toys on the livingroom floor. But what could happen if we don't pick them up? They could get broken. They could get lost. Someone might step on them and get a hurt foot. That's why we have pick them up. Let me help you. We'll pick up toys together." This way you are letting your child know that you understand how she feels. You are also helping her to understand why picking up toys is important. And you are letting her know she can count on you to be a partner in a hard job. You can turn clean-up times into teaching times. Say, "Where do the trucks go?" or "Let's pick up all the dirty clothes and put them in the hamper. Down they go!"

Try giving your child a choice. Say, "Do you want to pick up the red pieces or the blue pieces? You decide." This is called a *forced choice*. Your child still has to clean up so you get what you want, but your child gets to do it his way. Young children need to feel *independent* some of the time. They need to feel like they can *decide* about some things. Giving them choices makes them feel like they have some power. Feeling powerful is very important for children. It helps them to feel good about themselves.

When you can find ways to handle problems without yelling, you are helping to build a more loving and a more respectful relationship for you and your child.

What To Do When You've Had All You Can Take

Raising a child is hard work. It's a 24-hours-a-day job. Most of the time you have other things to do like cooking, cleaning, shopping, errands, and work outside of your home. Some days you may be so tired that you just feel angry. Before you lash out at your child, think about *why* you are angry. Is it because you haven't had a good night's sleep in weeks? Maybe

When you explain rules calmly and simply,
baby is much more likely to do what you want.

you had an awful day at work where people were
acting nasty or rude. Perhaps you had to stand in line
too long at the grocery store and then come home and
make dinner. Those reasons aren't your child's fault,
but they can really make you feel cranky.

Sometimes you feel like you've had all you can
take and are just tired out. Take a moment for yourself. Tell your three or four year-old, "I'm feeling
worn out! I need to rest by myself for 5 minutes, and
then we'll play together. You go color with your crayons or build a block castle while I rest, honey." Try to
give your child a hug or a smile to let him know that

you are not angry with him, and you are not rejecting him. Make sure you play with him or check in on him in five minutes as you said you would. You read all about promises in chapter 7. You know that your promises are precious words to your child.

There are some activities that babies and toddlers can do by themselves. While you sit down and rest, try putting your baby on a blanket on the floor beside you with some stand-up board books or pattern cards. Soft vinyl books and board books that stand up by themselves cost two or three dollars at most toy stores. Your baby can spend a few minutes looking at interesting pictures and designs. You might also try winding up a musical toy or putting on soft music for your baby. Lay baby on his back and let him play with items swinging from a mobile. Put baby on her tummy on a rug with safe toys close at hand.

Toddlers will enjoy looking through a stack of colorful books. You might try giving your toddler some blocks or toy cars or soft animals to play with. Another idea is to give your toddler a mound of playdough to squish and mold while you rest close by.

If you have a young toddler or baby and you cannot leave your child alone for a few minutes, then try to find other options. A playpen or a crib is a safe place to leave a baby while you go to another room to calm down. Could you call a friend, a neighbor, or someone in your family to come over for a few minutes? If you have a partner, trade off child care with each other.

If there is no place to go, then it's up to you to stay in control and not take your anger out on your child. If you have a baby swing, swing your baby for a few minutes while you calm down. Give your toddler one of the dump and pour games you've made from empty coffee cans and some rinsed out bottle caps from laundry detergent bottles. You could try to settle your child in his crib with an armful of books to entertain him.

Take a deep breath and count slowly to ten. People always say this, but it really works. Get a cold drink of water and wash your face as a refresher. Think of what you will do *for yourself* after your child is down for a nap or has gone to bed. Sometimes a piece of fruit or a cookie can pick up your mood. Baking cookies together with your toddler can give both of you a breather from fussing and an end product that tastes good.

Seeing the Difference Between Your Child and Your Child's Behavior

When you feel angry about something your child has done, try to *separate* who your *child* is from what your child *has done*. If your child spills a glass of red punch on your white shirt, what makes you angry? Is it really your child who has made your angry or the *behavior*, and the juice that was spilled? You feel angry because your white shirt is stained. Being upset with a behavior is a lot different from being upset with your child.

There are four big reasons a child misbehaves. The reasons are: 1) to get your attention, which he needs so much, 2) to feel more powerful, 3) to get revenge because he feels deeply hurt as if he cannot be loved, and 4) to act helpless so you won't nag or order him to do something he's afraid he'd fail at. A child may act out if he is angry, but remember that he has not yet learned a better way for dealing with his anger. The same thing is true for a child who acts out to get attention or power. Accidents happen because young children don't have control over their movements as grown-ups do. Young children are not able to plan carefully and figure out what will happen the way grown-ups can.

When accidents happen around the house, try to remember that children are not trying to do bad things on purpose to hurt you. Young children have a big struggle as they learn to control their bodies. They trip over things. They knock down things. They tip over glasses filled with juice because they are clumsy when they are young not because they deliberately want to make extra work for a papa or a mama. Children don't pay attention when juice glasses are tipping over in their hands the way grown-ups do.

If something happens that makes you really, really angry, you may need to take a break from the situation. It is better to take a breather for yourself. Take time-out rather than lose control, yell at, or hit your child. Use your words. Language helps you get control of the situation and lets your child understand how you feel. If something gets broken, and you're angry, try saying, "I'm really upset that the glass got broken. I know you didn't mean to break it. But that glass was a special present to me. I feel so angry that it is broken! I want to yell with a big, lion voice. I need to calm down for a minute, and then we'll talk about what happened." Catch your breath until you're in control and ready to talk. A good story to read about a little boy and his tired, frustrated mama is called *The Boy Who Could Make His Mother Stop Yelling* by Ilse Sondheimer.

How To Keep Accidents from Happening

Remember that young children are very "hands on." They want to touch and explore everything and everywhere. For instance, your toddler may take delight in unrolling all of the toilet paper from the roll. Instead of getting furious, think about what an adventurous, curious toddler you have. Put the toilet paper up high on the tank top for a few months. Give him old newspapers to tear and explain that toilet paper is for wiping bottoms and the paper you give him is for tearing. Two different actions with two different kinds of paper. Exploration and curious behavior like this mean that your toddler is smart and wants to learn.

Take a close look at your home. If there are things you don't want touched, move them out of your child's reach. Close the door to the bathroom firmly or put a latch up high on the door if you don't want your toddler going in there to dump toys in the toilet. Put your glass full of juice or cup of hot coffee on a high counter if you don't want it spilled. Put a new magazine in a high drawer if you don't want each page torn out. Learn how to *prevent* problems by *child-proofing* your house.

When something does happen, try to make the best of it. Try to make it a learning experience for your child. Model some language for your child. If your toddler has pulled a frozen food package and wrapper from your garbage bag, say, "You pulled that carton out of the trash. Now put it back in the trash bag. That belongs in the garbage." Try to have a sense of humor about your curious toddler who is so happy with his toy from the trash. Things will go easier for you and your child!

When You're Upset about Toilet Accidents

The same thing is true about toilet accidents. Toddlers don't wet their pants on purpose. You know that if your child's body is not ready to be toilet trained, *she can't help but have accidents.* Even when your child does know he needs to potty and he can tell you words like "poop" and "pee," he might have trouble *remembering* that he has to take his pants off first and then sit on the potty. This sounds simple to grown-ups, but young children have a hard time learning the sequence or order of activities. They can't remember what comes first or second and so on. Be patient with your child. Give him lots of gentle, clear, easy-to-understand reminders about what to do and what you expect. If you are a little person and afraid that your big folks will be angry at any toilet accidents, it is harder to learn to use a potty.

What To Do about Temper Tantrums

All children have temper tantrums. If tantrums happen in public you may be really angry. But below your anger, embarrassment may be the first thing you feel. When you feel embarrassed about your child's tantrum, keep in mind that *anyone* who has ever had children or been around children knows and understands that temper tantrums are just typical of toddlers and young children.

Even though you are feeling embarrassed and angry, try to understand the reasons behind the tantrum. Your child could be getting sick and not feeling well. He could be tired out. He could be frightened of something. There could be so much going around him that he is overloaded with stimulation. Perhaps he is being rushed around too fast from one place to another. If you are in a crowded shopping mall or a grocery store with lots of busy people, and moving carts, and things to look at and smell and hear, your child's temper tantrum may be saying, "Daddy, this is too much for me to handle. I'm too tired." You may be feeling too tired also. You might even wish somebody would carry you home! But you are the grown-up, and you can take charge of your feelings better than a baby can.

Here's a hint for the grocery store. Your child will probably see goodies she wants you to buy for her. Bring along something to keep her busy like an apple, some crackers, or a book. You could also tell her you will buy her one cookie or muffin from the store bakery. Some bakeries will even give free cookies to children. These kinds of treats will help prevent tantrums. Try to think of more "heading them off at the pass" ideas. You might explain to your child that if he waits with you while you are shopping for shoes, you will give him some playtime at the playground later in the day.

If your child sees a toy he really wants, let him know *you know* how he feels. You might say, "You really want that toy. You wish we could buy it. We aren't going to buy it, honey. But you can look at it and hold it for a while. Today we just have money to buy food for the house. We can play together when we get home with some of your toys." You can try to distract your child, after telling him you won't buy something, by giving him a job. Say, "Right now, I have a BIG job for you. I need to know how many things are in our cart. Please, count them for me so I know how much we're buying." Your child could help you look for the can with the picture of carrots or peas on the front. Give your child the special job of carefully holding the bananas so they don't bruise. Make the jobs sound really important. Thank your child for his help. Say, "I'm so glad you're shopping with me! You're a big help. Thank you!" He will beam. Your praise is like a dose of vitamins for your child's spirit. With these ideas you can make shopping a special learning time for you and your child.

Remember that children do not have the control over their emotions that adults do. They haven't learned how to control their feelings yet. Upset feelings spill out very easily in babies and young children.

23 Teach Your Child Words To Make Friends and Get Along with Other People

Understanding and practicing how to get along with other people is something children have to *learn*. Children are not born learning how to take turns or how to say magic words like "please," "Thank you," or "I'm sorry." They need a teacher, and *you* are your child's *first* and *most important teacher*. Children need practice as they learn social skills, and you can give them practice every day. Using language is a big part of the practice. Think of all the problems that could be solved between people if people would talk to each other instead of hitting or using angry words to hurt each other's feelings.

Think of situations that happen in your home everyday. Think of how you can use those situations to teach social skills. For instance, if one child grabs a piece of paper from another child, help the two children to talk about it. You might say, "Did you want a piece of paper?" The child nods. Ask the other child, "How did you feel when she grabbed your paper? Tell her how you felt." The child will probably say she felt sad or maybe scared or angry. Tell the child who grabbed the paper, "He felt so upset when you grabbed the paper. We know you want a piece of paper, but it's not OK to grab his paper. Here is another piece of paper you can use. Next time, come ask me for an extra piece of paper or ask your friend *if* he is willing to share." It takes a long time for young children to feel comfortable about sharing.

You want to try to help your child become aware of how other people feel. Young children need help learning how to understand other people's feelings and how to express their own feelings.

Help your child understand his feelings. Accept your child's feelings. If your child is afraid, don't scold him or call him a "scaredy-cat." Talk with your child about what has frightened him.

Spend time talking with your child about different emotions. Talk with your child about what makes him sad, happy, angry, scared, excited, and so on. If children feel you understand their feelings and they are taught to accept their own feelings, then they can more easily accept other people's feelings, too. You are a good model for accepting feelings even when you will not allow naughty or hurting behavior.

Your child will learn about feelings if *you* talk about *your* feelings. When you feel sad or happy, talk to your child about why you feel that way. Let your child see how you handle your emotions the best way you can.

Teach Your Child To Care about Other People

The main way you can help your child to care about other people is to show that you care about other people yourself. Remember that kids copy everything you do. They act the way you act. They will copy the tone of voice in which you talk to people or about people.

Scientists who have studied about what makes children care about other people, tell us that there are several things parents can do when bringing up a baby to help their baby become a caring, loving person from early on. First of all, you must strongly let your child know that hurting someone is *not* OK. You must show your child that you care if someone is hurt. Be firm but not harsh in disciplining your child. For example, if your child hits her younger sister on the head, say something like, "You must *never* hit a baby on the head. That hurts them. I *will not* let you hurt someone!" Show on your face and in your voice how upset you are.

Second, you can help your child learn to care by showing your love and concern to other people, especially your child and other family members. For instance, if one of your children is frightened by a barking dog, show a lot of concern for him. Say, "Oh, honey, that barking dog is scaring you. Let Mama hold you. I'll always keep you safe. Look, that doggie is behind his fence. He can't hurt you, but he sure is noisy! He just makes a lot of barking noise, doesn't he?" Wipe his eyes with a tissue. Give him a big hug. All of your actions and words send a loving message to your child: "I really care when you are hurt or scared. I will try to make you feel more comfortable and safe." If you make caring, loving kinds of behavior a routine in your house, chances are that you'll see your child copying your actions. Hopefully, you'll see your child patting your arm if you stub your toe or offering a tissue to a sad brother or sister or even trying, with real tenderness, to wipe the family dog's runny nose!

Keep in mind that being a caring person won't

make your child weak or wimpy. We all want to be around people who care about us and who are nice. The same thing is true for your child. Your child makes friends easier if he is a friendly, caring person.

When you are gentle with your child,
she can be gentle with others.

When you see your child showing concern for others, encourage that behavior. For example, imagine you and your child are walking down the street and your child sees another child crying while walking with his parent. Your child may say, "Why is that boy crying, Daddy?" You could say something like, "You noticed that he's sad. That's so nice of you to notice how other people are feeling. I don't know why he's sad. I hope he feels better soon."

If your child offers a hug to a brother or sister who's upset, say "You want to make your brother (or sister) feel better. Thank you for giving him such wonderful hug!"

The same thing is true for toys. Children especially act out familiar things with baby dolls. If your child is holding a baby doll and feeding him, say "You're being so gentle with your baby. He feels so safe when you hold him gently."

Teach Your Child the Magic Words

Everyone likes polite children. In school, teachers like polite children and other children like polite children. Teach your child "magic words" like *please* and *thank* you.

Once again, think about the powerful teacher you are for your child. Your child will copy what you do. When you ask for something, say "please." When someone gives you something, say "thank you." Make this a habit. When you talk to your child, model the magic words. Say things like, "Please put your toy away when you're finished." "Please hold your glass while I pour your milk." "Please hand me a napkin. Thank you."

When your child ask for more juice at breakfast, say "What's the magic word?" Remind your child to say "please." Then say, "When I hear you say "please," it really makes me want to help you." Do the same sort of thing for "thank you." Give your young child lots of practice. When you hand something to your toddler, say, "Thank you" for him. This will help him learn the word.

If you make using *please* and *thank you* an everyday part of talking, your child will grow up knowing the best way to talk with people. These kinds of *social skills* are really important in making friends and being well-liked. Don't worry that using *please* and *thank you* will make your child different from other children. Popular children are ones who know how to make their friends feel cared about and included. When you teach your child social skills, you are boosting the chance that your child will get along positively with his playmates. Both boys and girls need to learn these skills, and having these skills will make getting along with people later in life much easier.

Your child also needs to know some magic words in learning to play with other children. Once a group of young children were playing jump rope on a school playground. Another child came up and grabbed the rope, ran off and began jumping with it. No one had ever *taught* this child *how* to ask to play. Learning to play with others involves skills that you must *teach* your child. Think of how much easier things would have been for all of the children on that playground if the child who wanted to jump had said, "I love to jump rope. I'd like to jump, too. Can I have a turn too?"

You can teach your children how to play at home, in the park, or when a neighbor comes over to play. For instance, if you see your child grab a toy from a playmate, say to your child, "Hosea, if you want to have a turn playing, ask him: Can I please play with that?" Help your child understand what it means to *take turns*. Keep in mind that taking turns is really hard for toddlers and young children. Even if you tell them that they can have a turn in a minute, they may still be afraid that they'll never get to have a turn. If they give a toy to someone else for a turn, they may be afraid that they'll never see that toy again. Be patient with your child. Keep promises about when a child can have a turn. Keep reminding your child about turn-taking rules.

Try to give your child lots of examples of how to ask for things and how to play at home. You can do this when you're talking to your spouse, partner, friend, relative or anyone visiting. Try saying things like, "May I please see that newspaper when you're finished?" or "Jonathan, please help me dry these dishes?" or "Could you move over a little so I can sit on the sofa, too?" The idea is to help your child grow up in a family where he has lots of practice using language. If he's had practice in *how* to talk to people, then he'll have a much easier time getting along with people in school, in the neighborhood, and in your family. He will have special language power.

Social Time as Learning Time

Arrange some play times with other children and families. Not only will your child have hands-on practice using language, but she will learn how to interact with others.

Introducing babies to other babies and toddlers is a wonderful learning experience for your child. Especially with toddlers and very young children, be ready to help your child learn to play with others by supporting his efforts to play with a friend. For example, in playgroup a toddler, Harry, was sitting on the bed of a wooden toy truck. Noticing this, Natalie, another child, brought over her doll and placed the doll on the truck bed so that the doll could go for a ride. Harry moved the truck forward and the doll fell off. Natalie picked up her doll and walked away. An adult could have said something like, "Harry, Natalie put her doll on your truck. She would like you to take her doll for

Meeting another baby for the first time can be a wonder-filled experience and the beginning of making a friend.

a ride. Will you please take the baby for a ride? Thank you so much." Putting words to Natalie's actions helps Harry and Natalie play together.

Talking with toddlers and describing their actions to each other helps toddlers learn how to invite each other to play. Toddlers need your help to start playing in gentle and friendly ways with each other. If a toddler silently brings a block over to another child, that is her way of asking that child to play. You can say, "Lindsay gave you a block. See, she's building with blocks on the floor. She wants to build with her." Your words help young children learn to play together.

By playing together, toddlers and young children learn positive social skills like sharing and helping another who is hurt or sad. When you practice these kinds of skills at home, your child will repeat these skills with friends. A toddler who gently pats the head of a sad friend is copying the loving behavior he receives at home. Young toddlers who comfort an upset child or share food with a playmate show love and concern for others because their special adults show lots of love and care for them!

24 Things To Remember

Every Child Is Different

Be careful not to compare your child to other children. If you have several children, try not to compare them to each other. Each child has a distinct personality. If you have several children, you are probably noticing how different your children are every day! Every child is completely special and *unlike any other person on the entire earth.* That's pretty special. Children grow and learn at different rates. Remember to be patient as your child grows and learns. You can provide lots of interesting learning experiences and lots of practice using his new skills, but your child must learn at his own pace. Learning to live in the world is a hard thing! Each baby has to learn so much that is brand new. You can help your child most by being loving and warm. Let your child know *every day* that you're so happy to be her Mama or Daddy. You can do this by being a happy, loving parent. Give your child lots of hugs, smiles, and encouragement. Notice her small successes, and let her know how proud you are.

When These Games Just Aren't Working

There will be days when you feel so frustrated with being a parent. That's OK and it's perfectly normal. Try to puzzle out what is so frustrating to you.

Express your pleasure as your baby learns even
a simple game like shaking a rattle.

try to figure out a way to make things easier. Always
remember, though, that your child needs your love.

If you're trying to play games you've learned about
with your child, and he doesn't want to play, that's
OK. Maybe he's tired or not feeling well. Be aware of
your child's moods because that really affects what
you play together and how you play together. If a
game isn't working, leave it and try again later.

25 Finding the Gifts of Your Child

You know your child better than anyone. You know the little things that make your child so special. Find those special abilities and interests, those *gifts* in your child. Everyone has something that sets that person apart from everyone else. Some gifts might be:

- a twinkling smile that makes you feel great to be a parent
- a wonderful imagination
- telling stories
- saying cute things
- giving big hugs
- drawing
- talking
- knowing numbers
- being a caring person
- mannerisms (special things your child does, like the way she grins or the way he scratches his head when he thinks)
- playing special games with you
- singing in tune
- being a great helper to you
- being tender and entertaining as a big brother or sister
- remembering rhymes

Take some time to find the *gifts* of your child. The gifts are there!

When you are kind and giving, your kids will copy you.

You have your own gifts, too! Think about the special abilities in you that will make you a great parent. Think about the kind of life you want your child to have. Think about how you can help your child to have that life. If there were things you didn't like from your childhood, *now* is the time to change them. Maybe you didn't get enough hugs. Maybe you got spanked too much. Maybe no one ever taught you how to use words to tell how you felt. Maybe you felt like no one really ever understood you. Take some time, and think about when you were a child. Let yourself feel angry or sad about the things you didn't like. Say to yourself, "Things are going to be different for my child!" Do everything you can to make life better and more loving for you and your child.

You have a big job ahead of you, but you can do it! You are a special person. Find those special qualities. Find all of the love you can to give to your child. Use the *power* of language. You can help your child to learn to feel good about being a special person who knows how to get along with others, and how to be successful in learning and later on in school. As your child grows learning the power of language and feeling safe and happy with you, the wonderful thing is that you'll get all of that love right back as your child grows up!

Other Good Books To Boost Your Baby's Language

Allison, C. 1991. *I'll Tell You a Story, I'll Sing You a Song. A Parent's Guide to Fairy Tales, Fables, Songs, and Rhymes of Childhood*. New York: Delta.

Barton, B. 1986. *Tell Me Another. Storytelling and Reading Aloud at Home, at School and in the Community*. Markham, Ontario: Pembroke.

Beck, M. S. 1979. *Baby Talk. How Your Child Learns To Speak*. New York: Plume.

DeVine, M. 1991. *Baby Talk: The Art of Communicating with Infants and Toddlers*. New York: Plenum.

Elligson, D. K. 1966. *Seals, Sea Gulls and Other Sounds*. Chicago: Systems for Education.

Fowler, W. 1990. *Talking from Infancy. How To Nurture and Cultivate Early Language Development*. Cambridge, Mass.: Brookline Books.

Holzman, M. 1983. *The Language of Children. Development in Home and School*. Englewood Cliffs, N.J.: Prentice-Hall.

Honig, A. S. 1982. *Playtime Learning Games for Young Children*. Syracuse: Syracuse Univ. Press.

Ross, M. J. M. 1982. *Read To Me! Teach Me! A Complete Reference Guide to Books for Fun and Early Learning*. Wauwatosa, Wisc.: American Baby Books.

References

Berko-Gleason, J. 1993. "Studying Language Development: An Overview and a Preview." In *The Development of Language,* edited by J. Berko-Gleason, pp. 1–35. New York: Macmillan.

Blank, M., and F. Solomon 1968. "How Shall the Disadvantaged Be Taught?" *Child Development* 39:47–62.

Bryant, J. 1983. *Children's Understanding of Television: Research on Attention and Comprehension.* New York: Academic.

Bryant, J. 1990. *Television and the American Family.* Hillsdale, N.J.: L. Erlbaum.

Clarke-Stewart, K. A. 1973. "Interactions Between Mothers and Their Young Children: Characteristics and Consequences. *Monographs of the Society for Research in Child Development* 38 (serial no. 153).

DeCasper, A., and M. Spence. 1986. "Prenatal Maternal Speech Influences Newborns' Perception of Speech Sounds." *Infant Behavior and Development* 9:133–50.

DeVine, M. 1991. *Baby Talk: The Art of Communicating with Infants and Toddlers.* New York: Plenum.

Dinkmeyer, D., and G. D. McKay. 1982. *The Parent's Handbook: Systematic Training for Effective Parenting.* Circle Pines, Minn.: American Guidance Service.

Fraiberg, S., E., Adelson, and V. Shapiro. 1987. "Ghosts in the Nursery: A Psychoanalytic Approach to the Problems of Impaired Infant-Mother Relationships." In *Selected Writings of Selma Fraiberg,* edited by L. Fraiberg. Columbus: Ohio State Univ. Press.

Friedlander, B., et al. 1972. "Time Sampling Analysis of Infants' Natural Language Environments in the Home." *Child Development* 43:730–40.

Greenspan, S., and N. T. Greenspan. 1986. *First Feelings:*

Milestones in the Emotional Development of Your Baby and Child. New York: Penguin.

Healy, J. 1989. *Your Child's Growing Mind: A Guide to Learning and Brain Development from Birth to Adolescence.* New York: Doubleday.

Healy, J. 1990. *Endangered Minds: Why Children Don't Think and What We Can Do about It.* New York: Touchstone.

Honig, A. S. 1982. *Playtime Learning Games for Young Children.* Syracuse: Syracuse Univ. Press.

Honig, A. S. 1985. "The Art of Talking to a Baby." *Working Mother,* 8, no. 3:72–78.

Honig, A. S. 1988. "Research in Review: Humor Development in Children." *Young Children,* 43, no. 4:60–73.

Honig, A. S. 1993. "Toilet Learning." *Day Care and Early Education* 21, no. 1:6–9.

Honig, A. S. 1995. "Singing with Infants and Toddlers." *Young Children* 50, no. 5:72–78.

Honig, A. S. 1996. *Developmentally Appropriate Behavior Guidelines for Infants and Toddlers from Birth to Three Years.* Little Rock, Ark.: Southern Early Childhood Assoc.

Honig, A. S., and J. R. Lally, 1972. *Infant Caregiving: A Design for Training.* Syracuse: Syracuse Univ. Press.

Norton, D. E. 1991. *Through the Eyes of a Child: An Introduction to Children's Literature.* 3d ed. New York: Merrill.

Pflaum, S. W. 1986. *The Development of Language and Literacy in Young Children.* 3d ed. Columbus, Ohio: Charles Merrill.

Pines, M. 1979. Good Samaritans at Age Two? *Psychology Today* 13, no. 1:66–77.

Singer, D. G. 1981. *Teaching Television: How To Use TV to Your Child's Advantage.* New York: Dial.

Singer, J. L. 1981. *Television, Imagination, and Aggression: A Study of Preschoolers.* Hillsdale, N.J.: L. Erlbaum.

Tough, J. 1974. *Talking, Thinking, Growing.* New York: Schocken.